HUT TO HUT IN
THE STUBAI ALPS

Sulzenau Hut to the Dresdener Hut via the Peiljoch: negotiating fixed ropes

HUT TO HUT
IN THE
STUBAI ALPS

Walking the popular
Stubai Rucksack Route and
the Stubai Glacier Tour

by
ALLAN HARTLEY

CICERONE PRESS
MILNTHORPE, CUMBRIA

© Allan Hartley
ISBN 1 85284 123 0

British Cataloguing-in-Publication Data. A catalogue record for this book
is available from the British Library.

Advice to Readers

Readers are advised that whilst every effort is taken by the
author to ensure the accuracy of this guidebook, changes
can occur which may affect the contents. It is advisable to
check locally on transport, accommodation, shops etc but
even rights-of-way can be altered and, more especially
overseas, paths can be eradicated by landslip, forest fires or
changes of ownership.
The publisher would welcome notes of any such changes.

Slight variations in the spelling of place names may occur
throughout this book.

Front Cover: Wilderpfaff and Zuckerhutl from the Grosser Trögler

CONTENTS

Introduction

Topography 7
Getting to Austria: By road; By rail; By air 7
Accommodation in the valley: Hotels; Campsites 8
Innsbruck: Important sights and locations 9
The Austrian Alpine Club 10
Meals and provisions 13
Currency 15
Kit and equipment 16
Maps 16
Route descriptions and sketch maps 17
Route grading 17
Standard times 18
Route finding 18
Seasonal change 18
Children 19
Altitude 19
Glacier travel: Glaciers and crevasse rescue techniques ...19
Mountain rescue and insurance 23
Language: Mountain terminology; Useful words and phrases 24
Huts: Descriptions and locations 26

The Stubai Rucksack Route

General introduction 43
Altitudes 44
Route summary 45
Route descriptions and sketch maps 46

The Stubai Glacier Tour

General introduction 89
Route summary 90
Altitudes 91
Route descriptions and sketch maps 92

INTRODUCTION

TOPOGRAPHY

The Stubai Alps are situated south-west of the old Austrian city of Innsbruck, in the province of the Tyrol. The area has no access difficulties and is easily reached by local transport from Innsbruck in about one hour.

Generally, the main peaks of the Stubai, Wilder Freiger, Zuckerhütl chain straddle the border with Italy and embrace the area known as the South Tyrol, referring to previous Austrian territory annexed to Italy after World War I.

The boundary of the Stubai is generally recognised as the Brenner Pass to the east, the Sölden valley in the Ötztal to the west, the mountains of the Italian South Tyrol to the south and the Inn valley to the north.

The Stubai's highest mountain is the Zuckerhütl at 3505m, with a further 130 peaks over 3000m, many of which are glaciated.

GETTING TO AUSTRIA

By road

The most direct route is via the Dover-Ostend channel crossing, then to make use of the motorway system to Munich and into Austria at Kufstein, followed by the short drive up the Inn valley to Innsbruck.

Tour plans and route descriptions are available through the RAC and AA motoring organisations who will advise of any toll road charges en route.

By rail

There is a regular train service across Europe most days of the week. British Rail International Service will advise of possible routes, such as Ostend - Brussels - Munich - Innsbruck, or Calais - Paris - Innsbruck.

Travel time is approximately twenty-four hours from London.

By air

Daily flights to Munich by British Airways from London and Manchester take a little less than two hours. From Munich a regular bus service connects with the main railway station, from where a frequent train service to Innsbruck is about two hours.

Alternatively, Dan Air operate a limited service from Gatwick (London) direct to Innsbruck.

ACCOMMODATION IN THE VALLEY

Hotels

A vast array of hotel accommodation is available throughout the medieval city of Innsbruck to cater for all tastes and budgets. Hotels may be booked in advance by obtaining a hotel list from the UK Section of the Austrian Alpine Club, or be booked on arrival in Innsbruck at the Tourist Information Centre at the railway station. (See Innsbruck street map.)

Hotels in Neustift tend to cater for the tourist trade, but there are an abundance of guest houses and small hotels where climbers and walkers will feel more at home! As with the hotels in Innsbruck, advance booking may be made via the Tourist Information Centre in Innsbruck or Neustift.

Campsites

Innsbruck

Several campsites exist within a short distance of the city. There are two sites at Kranebitten a few kilometres west of the airport and two more on the east of the city, one at Reichenau and one at Amras.

Neustift

Good campsites exist at Madrager Stille in the hamlet of Madras, south of Fulpmes and at Volderau, south-west of Neustift. Anyone intending to camp should enquire from the campsite warden about reduced fees whilst they are away: these are referred to as *leeres Zelt*.

diagram of Innsbruck

The River Inn

Goldenes Dachl; The Golden Roof. Ornate royal box built by Emperor Maximilian I in 1500. The roof of which is covered in gold plated tiles.

To Kufstein & the German border

The old part of the city & square contains many fine examples of architectural styles & includes the Imperial Palace (Hofburg) & City Tower (Stadturm).

Museum Strasse

The Austrian Alpine Club headquarters & Alpine Museum. (Open Monday to Friday during normal business hours.)

The "Old City" & Square

To the airport

Hauptbahnhof (Railway station)

Information Centre

Bus stop for Stubaital

Bus Station

Maria Theresien Strasse; Statue of Annasaule, St Anna's column. Erected in 1706 in thanksgiving for the successful defence against Bavarian invasion during the war of Spanish Succession.

Triumphforte; Triumphal Arch in memory of Emperor Franz I

To the Stubai; the Brenner Pass & Italy

9

THE AUSTRIAN ALPINE CLUB

The Österreichischer Alpenverein (Ö.A.V.) was founded in 1862 to foster and encourage the sport of mountaineering. Presently the club has over 200,000 members of all age groups, embracing all facets of mountaineering. Membership is open to any person without exception, who has a love of the mountains regardless of age or ability.

The club's principal activities include development and provision of mountain huts, marking and maintenance of footpaths, the production of guidebooks and maps, the organising of mountaineering courses, tours and expeditions. In addition, the club is becoming increasingly involved in environmental issues, particularly those which are seen to spoil the mountains by either physical or visual pollution.

Club members enjoy reciprocal rights agreements with all the other major alpine clubs: in France (CAF) Switzerland (CAS), Italy (CIA) and Germany (DAV).

The English section was formed in 1948 to make it easier for British mountaineers to visit and travel throughout the Eastern Alps. Today the English section is one of the largest UK mountaineering clubs. It organises its own activities by having a regular outdoor/indoor meets programme, together with the publication of a quarterly newsletter and also runs tours and courses for its members in Austria.

Anyone intending to undertake a hut-to-hut tour anywhere in Austria is strongly recommended to join the English section by applying to:

The Secretary
The Austrian Alpine Club
13 Longcroft House
Fretherne Road
WELWYN GARDEN CITY
Herts AL8 6PQ   (0707 324835)

Apart from the very real benefit of enjoying preferential treatment and reduced costs at the huts, perhaps the main advantage of being a member is that of "belonging". This feeling of friendliness - greatly cherished and fostered by everyone - will be experienced many times when various huts are visited, particularly over a number of years. It is referred to as *gemütlich!*

Huts

Whilst "hut" is frequently used throughout the guidebook, it is not what the word implies: mountain inn would be a more appropriate description for these wonderful buildings. Collectively there are well over a thousand huts in Austria, half of which are owned by the Austrian and German Alpine Club. In the Stubai there is a total of 30 ÖAV - DAV huts, most of which are open from the beginning of July to mid-September. All the huts in the Stubai have a resident guardian, usually a guide *(Bergführer)* and his family. Each hut has simple sleeping accommodation in the form of mixed dormitories *(Matratzenlager)* with blankets and pillows, and perhaps a number of bedrooms with blankets, duvet and sheets.

Sometimes when the huts are full, bed space will be found in the winter room. This is where logs are stored and can be quite cosy but remember to store your kit off the floor as it is usually home for the huts' permanent four-pawed residents. Alternatively bed space will be found in the dining room and along various corridors. This is known as *Nottlager*, but sleeping with the furniture is a more apt description.

In all instances visitors should provide their own cotton sheet sleeping bags. These are now becoming compulsory to help save water and fuel and reduce the effects of detergents polluting water courses downstream of the huts. So its seems likely that bed linen will be phased out and blankets only will become the norm.

In addition to sleeping accommodation each hut will have some form of restaurant service offering a number of tradition Austrian dishes (see Meals and provisions). The menu generally comprises soup, a choice of main meals, *Bergsteigeressen*, cold meats, cheese, and sometimes cakes and sweets. All huts serve drinks, tea, coffee, beer, wine, and so forth, most huts have a small shop where visitors can buy chocolate and biscuits. Post cards may be purchased and posted at the hut. The post is usually taken down the valley once a week and handed in at the main post office. Post to UK this way normally takes 10/14 days.

Each hut will have some form of wash and toilet facilities which vary from being excellent - Franz Senn, Amberger, Sulzenau huts - more modest at the Bremer or be quite primitive like the Müller Hut. However, it does seem likely that the provision of hot water at some huts will gradually diminish as the club moves towards more simple and basic necessities and tries to do its bit to preserve the use of fuel and water.

Elsewhere in the hut, usually near the front door, is the *Trockenraum*, or the drying room, where wet clothes can be dried.

The main room at all huts is the *Gaststube* or common room, which also doubles as the dining room. It is here where the day's events are reviewed, routes planned, meals enjoyed, birthdays celebrated, games played, songs sung and all manner of activity that goes into fostering camaraderie - that is *gemütlich!!*

At the hut

On arrival at the hut, you should first remove your boots and store them in the boot rack which will be close to the front door. You should also hang your ice axe, crampons and rope on the racks provided. Ice axes and crampons are not permitted in the dormitories and bedrooms. If you are wet on arrival, your waterproofs should be shaken as dry as possible outside and hung up with your ice tackle. If you are in a group, do not mill around the doorway and again if you are wet make sure your group leaves its surplus water and as much as possible dirt off boots outside. Many of the huts are spotless, and obviously for the benefit of all guests like to remain that way.

You should then establish contact with the housekeeper - usually the *Bergführer's* wife, to obtain your overnight accommodation. A maximum of three consecutive nights is the club rule, but this is not generally rigidly enforced. You will usually find this most important person in the kitchen *(Küche)* or in the dining room *(Gaststube)*. Having found her, it is important to greet her by saying *Grüs Gott* , and then to explain that you (and if you have a group with you) are members of the UK section of the Austrian Alpine Club and that you would like some accommodation. The lady will usually ask to see your membership card and maybe retain it overnight or until such time as you leave, when you will be asked to pay.

If you do not speak German or feel uncomfortable with asking for rooms in German, then write down the phrase noted in the language section of this guide. Be polite by asking *bitte* when handing her the message and thanking her *danke* when she gives it back. Trivial as these polite gestures may seem, they are extremely important, and if practised will go a long way to ensuring a pleasant stay.

On departure, remember to fold your blankets, to look round and ensure nothing is forgotten, and finally to search out the housekeeper and thank her for a pleasant stay. You should also remember to collect your club card if it has not been given back to you, and you should complete the hut book to record your stay and indicate where you will be going next.

MEALS AND PROVISIONS

As previously mentioned, all huts have some sort of restuarant service to cover the three main daily meals; breakfast *(Frühstück)*, lunch *(Mittagessen)* and dinner *(Abendessen)*.

Breakfast is served from about 0600hrs to approx 0730hrs. Therefafter no meals are available until lunch time as the hut staff are busy with general housekeeping. Breakfast is seen as the worst value for money but unless you carry your own provisions you will have little choice other than to accept it.

Lunchtime is usually from 1200 to 1400hrs but varies depending on the hut. However, it is possible to purchase simple meals like soup, *Käse Brot, Apfelstrüdl* at most huts throughout the afternoon.

Dinner is the main meal of the day and is generally served from 1800hrs to 1900hrs. Apart from meals on the menu *Bergsteigeressen* will be available along with the other evening meals. Literally translated it means mountain climbers' food and in reality that is what it is, even if it is pot luck what you get! However, it is low priced and must contain a minimum of 500 calories. The meal generally comprises spaghetti or pasta, potatoes, some meat or sausage, other vegetables, sometimes a fried egg or maybe a dumpling. There is no hard and fast rule other than that it is relatively inexpensive and that there's usually a lot of it.

Generally the procedure for ordering meals is that you first organise a table. There is no formality, but sometimes when courses are being run, groups of tables may be marked private or reserved *privat reservierung*. Having sat down one of the waitresses *(Fraüline)* will take your order.

Alternatively you may have to go to the counter and ask to order or there may be a sign *selbstbedienungs* which means self-service.

The general rule for paying for food and drink is to pay an accumulative bill. Therefore visitors are advised to make notes of their consumpton to aid checking at the time of paying. Take note, these lists can be considerable when staying at a hut more than a couple of nights.

Because of the excellent service the huts provide it is obvious that very little of one's own food need to be carried. However, many people do bring with them their own dry rations: tea, coffee, bread, cheese etc. This permits them to make their own snacks and, by purchasing *Teewasser* and borrowing cups, allows them the opportunity to brew up for a small cost.

The only facility not provided for is self-catering - and it does seem a little pointless when all the meals are reasonably priced. Most drinks - tea, coffee, chocolate, cola, lemonade, beer, wine and schnapps are available at the huts.

Selected menu list

Breakfast - *Frühstück*
2/3 slices of bread, portion of butter and jam, tea, coffee or chocolate.

Mittag & Arbendessen	*Main Meals*
Wiener Schnitzel	Breaded veal fillets
Jäger Schnitzel	Stuffed slices of beef often wrapped in bacon
Tyroler Grötzl	Fried potato and eggs
Spiegeleier und schinken	Fried eggs and bacon
Gulasch	Cube meat in rich sauce
Zweibelrostbraten	Broiled beef and onions
Wurst Brot	Sausage and bread
Käse Brot	Cheese and bread
Schinken Brot	Ham and bread
Bergsteigeressen	Special 'climbers' meal' provided cheaply by huts

Kaiserschmarren	Sweet pancakes
Tagessuppe	Soup of the day
Knödelsuppe	Soup with dumplings
Wurstsuppe	Soup with sausages
Apfelstrudel	Apple pie
Compote	Tinned fruit

Meals are usually served with a selection of vegetables or salad. For those who don't speak German the following vocabulary associated with eating may prove useful.

Speisekarte	Menu
Tasse	Cup
Teller	Plate
Schüssel	Bowl
Messer	Knife
Gabel	Fork
Löffel	Spoon
Bröt/Brötchen	Bread/rolls
Kartoffeln	Potato
Gemüse	Vegetables
Salt	Salt
Pfeffer	Pepper
Senf	Mustard
Reis	Rice

CURRENCY

The unit of currency in Austria is the Schilling. For calculating budget costs, a price list for the huts can be obtained from the UK Section of the Austrian Alpine Club. Alternatively a budget cost can be calculated on the basis of prices charged in most English pubs for a decent bar meal. Similarly for drinks. Exchange rates fluctuate but are given in some newspapers, banks and travel bureaux.

KIT AND EQUIPMENT

Stubai Rucksack Route

Depending on personal preference, a general kit list would comprise rucksack, boots (plus dubbin), two pairs of long socks, snow gaiters, waterproofs, breeches, two shirts, pullover, sun hat, balaclava, scarf, mittens, change of underwear, water bottle, torch (with spare battery and bulb), whistle, map, compass, guidebook, note pad, pencils, pocket knife, first aid kit, sun-glasses, sun cream, lip salve, small towel, toilet bag, sewing kit, a selection of polythene bags, bivvy bag and emergency food rations.

Since snow will be encountered, walkers should equip themselves with an ice axe or a pair of ski sticks. Optional extras include German phrase book, camera and films and altimeter.

However, if it is the party's intention to try the mountains of the Habicht, Feuerstein, Wilder Freiger, Schaufelspitze, Lisenser Ferner Kogel, the kit list should include ice axe, crampons, set of Prusik loops, two long tape slings with karabiners, climber's harness and a minimum of 30mx9mm climbing rope. It is also important to have the ability to use this kit.

Stubai Glacier Tour

General kit list as mentioned above, and the following additional items are required by each member of the group: ice axe, crampons, set of Prusik loops, one ice screw, one universal rock peg, two long tape slings with karabiners, climber's harness, two spare karabiners. Plus, for each group of three people, 45mx9mm climbing rope, one dead man snow belay, a selection of about six slings and one peg hammer. Other items which are useful but not essential are ice hammer, figure of eight abseil device, Prusik device such as Petzl-Jumar.

MAPS

The following maps are required for both the Stubai Rucksack Route and the Stubai Glacier Tour. The maps are published by the Austrian Alpine Club and are available from the UK section.

Sheet 31/1	1:25,000	Stubai Alpen: Hoch Stubai
Sheet 31/2	1:25,000	Stubai Alpen: Sellrain

Bremer Hut

Bremer Hut, Schneespitze on the left, Pflerscher Hoch Joch on the right

Hoch Stubai Hut

Also recommended, since the map covers the complete regions at a glance:

Sheet 83   1:50,000   Kompass Wanderkarte. Stubai Alpen: Serleskamm.

ROUTE DESCRIPTIONS AND SKETCH MAPS

Throughout the text, each daily tour itinerary is fully described and illustrated with a sketch map indicating the main topographical features en route. Abbreviations used are as follows:

R100	route number
Δ	summit cairn
†	summit cross
SP	signpost
FR	fixed ropes
B	bridge
H	bus stop
gl/fr	glacier/ferner
sch/jl	Scharte/Jochl
?	caution: loose ground crevasses etc
*	panoramic viewpoint
N,S,E,W	north, south, east, west

ROUTE GRADING

Both the routes described are for people who are already involved in some form of mountain activity on a regular basis. It goes without saying that you should be in good health and physically fit.

The Stubai Rucksack Route is a moderately strenuous tour involving days of continuous walking, carrying a full pack for an average of six hours a day. Each day will involve the negotiation of steep ground, some of which will require scrambling ability and some of which will be protected by fixed wire ropes to aid stability. Patches of old snow are also likely to be encountered on north-facing hillsides and in gullies.

The Stubai Glacier Tour is a strenuous tour demanding stamina and experience. In terms of alpine grading the route falls within the easy to moderate category and comprises steep walking, sustained

17

scrambling, steep snow slopes and crevassed glaciers. Both routes demand that participants should have a good head for heights.

STANDARD TIMES

At the beginning of each route description a standard time in hours is quoted as an estimate of the time required from hut to hut. This standard time generally equates to that given in the Austrian Alpine Club's Hut Book. The standard time stated is for the hours spent moving and does not include lunch stops and other breaks. Most British parties find some difficulty in meeting "standard" times. This is of no consequence since quite a few standard times are unattainable anyway. With this in mind, the route descriptions in this book also quote the "actual" time required in the body of the text.

Participants undertaking the Rucksack Route with children are advised to add at least one hour to the standard time to allow for frequent picnic stops. Similarly aspirant alpinists on the glacier tour should make due allowance to the standard time, whilst they learn the rudiments of glacier travel and the time-consuming activity of putting crampons on and roping up.

ROUTE FINDING

Most of the routes described are on recognised mountain paths and tracks normally identified with red waymarks or stone cairns. All paths have an identification number which corresponds to those indicated on maps and signposts. Where the route follows a stream, river or glacier, reference is made to left and right bank viewed in the direction of flow. This means that in ascent the left bank will be on the right.

SEASONAL CHANGE

The recommended time to undertake the tour is between mid-July to mid-September. In July there is likely to be more snow at low altitude than in September. Whilst less snow will be an advantage on the Rucksack Route, minimal snow can be a real disadvantage on the Glacier Tour. The weather is generally settled from July to September, but summer storms do occur and this means that both routes are subject to snowfall during adverse weather.

CHILDREN

Throughout the guidebook, there are a number of references to children undertaking the Rucksack Route. By way of definition, it is highly unlikely that children under the age of ten would have sufficient stamina to undertake some of the long walks such as the Innsbrucker-Bremer, Dresdner-Neue Regensberger hut connections. However, should the youngsters be capable of say Snowdon or Helvellyn and are keen to be in the mountains for long periods at a time they will probably be OK, but only the parents can decide.

ALTITUDE

In general the average altitude embraced by both tours is between 2500m and 3000m (8000 to 10,000 feet). See altitude diagrams.

Providing participants are physically fit, it is unlikely that the effects of altitude sickness will become apparent other than a bit of puffing and panting.

GLACIERS AND GLACIER TRAVEL: CREVASSE RESCUE TECHNIQUES

Overall the glaciers of the Stubai tend to be relatively small and compact in comparison to glaciers of the Zillertal, Ötztal, and Venediger.

Whilst crevasses exist and will be encountered most do not create a problem for the mountain traveller and most are easily bypassed. As is common to most glaciers, the main crevasse zones will be on steep sections, at the edges and where the ice breaks away from the underlying rocks to form *Bergschrunds*. If difficulties do arise it will be in negotiating *Bergschrunds* such as may exist below the Wildgrat Scharte and below the Wilder Freiger on the Übeltal glacier.

Orientation on the glaciers is described as being in the direction of flow along the right or left bank. In ascent, this means that the left bank will be on your right. To avoid confusion, as may exist when route finding in mist, a compass bearing has been added.

Whilst most of the Stubai glaciers are relatively straightforward, they can vary quite considerably season to season. This is further exacerbated by temperature and because of the glaciers' relative low altitude. This means that whilst routes may be straightforward one year, with minimal winter snowfall, previously hidden crevasses may become exposed and enlarged. Therefore glacier travel becomes more problematic.

The ideal number of people for safe glacier travel is four. Two is the absolute minimum, but they cannot be entirely safe, and solo travel should be avoided for obvious reasons. For a party of two, some added security can be gained by teaming up with a second party, gaining strength through weight of numbers.

Many of the Stubai's glaciers are dry glaciers at their lower levels, and are initially quite safe to traverse un-roped as the crevasses are obvious and easily avoided.

However, when crevasses pose a threat, for example, where they overlap, are deep, and when they occur on steep ground, then the party should be roped. Equally parties should be roped at all times whilst traversing glaciers that are snow-covered as will be found on say the Wütenkar and Sulzenau glaciers, no matter how well trodden the route is. It is worth remembering that crevasses have no respect for people and can open up beneath the best of us.

For a roped party of three, the leader of the group is best placed last, since it is the leader who will contribute most in the event of a mishap. The leader's second should take the lead position on the rope so as to route find and the last person should take up a place in the middle.

For parties of equal ability and for those visiting the Alps for the first time, some experimenting will be necessary to gain more experience. The following is suggested as a way of ensuring the group has a safe anchor man at all times.

In ascent and descent the lightest person should go at the front to route find. Should the leader fall into a crevasse (unlikely) it is very unlikely that the rest of the party would be dragged with him.

Should a mishap occur then the heaviest person at the back is best placed to act as anchor man. For a party of two the most experienced person should be the back man in ascent and descent.

For a party of three to rope up, the middle man should tie on in the middle, the anchor man should tie on about 12m behind him, and the leader, who needs a bit more rope should tie on about 15m in front. The surplus rope at both ends should be coiled and carried over the shoulder, then it can be used in the event of crevasse rescue.

In addition to roping up, three Prusik loops need attaching to the rope then stored in one's pockets. A clove hitch should also be tied around the head of each person's ice axe to allow instant belays. On normal glaciers the party will move together keeping a respectable distance between each person. Rope coils may be carried by each person to prevent the rope snagging and being dragged along the glacier surface.

When crevassed zones are encountered, the rope between individuals should be taut to limit the effect of a fall. Where crevasses pose a very real risk, such as when they are large or their extent is unknown, the leader's second should belay, whilst the leader traverses or jumps the crevasse. At the same time the group's actual leader will be similarly belayed, some distance away as the group's anchor man. Whilst the procedures may seem complicated and time-consuming, with a little practice they should become second nature.

The purpose behind these techniques is to prevent climbers falling in crevasses and to ensure glaciers are safely crossed. Most mountaineers will spend many hours crossing glaciers without any serious mishap. Experienced mountaineers will be able to recall falling into crevasses up to the waist, a few to the chest and the odd one falling through the surface to the glacier below. In most instances during a fall the climber can react quickly enough to spread his weight by outstretching his arms or by falling backwards to prevent falling further. Once the fall is arrested, his second should belay whilst the anchor man uses the spare rope to haul him free.

Should the leader fall free and end up inside the crevasse, it is important the rest of the party work quickly. It is likely the leader will have hurt himself if he has fallen into a concealed crevasse. This is due to the fact that his rucksack will jar, pushing the head forward

Crevasse Rescue Techniques

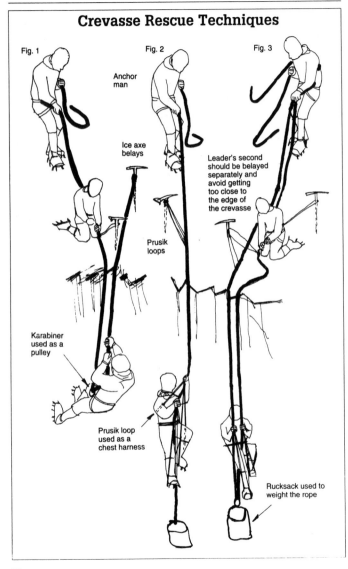

Fig. 1

Fig. 2

Fig. 3

Anchor man

Ice axe belays

Leader's second should be belayed separately and avoid getting too close to the edge of the crevasse

Prusik loops

Karabiner used as a pulley

Prusik loop used as a chest harness

Rucksack used to weight the rope

and banging it on the ice during the fall. In such a situation there are a number of options to choose from, but all will be useless unless the group has spent a little time practising crevasse rescue techniques.

In this situation, provided the leader is uninjured it may be possible:

a) Simply to haul him out of the crevasse using Prusik loops to lock off the rope between each haul (fig. 1).
b) The leader may be able to Prusik out of the crevasse under his own steam (fig. 2).
c) By lowering the end of the rope the leader can be rescued by using a combination of hauling and Prusiking (fig. 3).

If the leader is injured, the middle man will have to go into the crevasse to perform first aid and secure the second haulage rope. Thereafter once back on the surface it is just about possible for his two companions to haul him to the surface, using Prusik loops to lock off the rope.

MOUNTAIN RESCUE AND INSURANCE

Both routes involve sustained activity in a mountain environment. Inevitably this increases the risk of an accident taking place. This means that a severe fall, breaking of a limb or some other serious mishap will result in the mountain rescue team being called out.

Apart from the distress caused to the injured person, the cost of mounting a rescue operation is considerable, particularly when helicopters are involved and this will have to be paid for by the person being rescued.

Whilst membership of the Austrian Alpine Club includes a nominal amount of insurance for rescue purposes, it is recommended that additional insurance is taken out by each person.

Insurance may be arranged through the Austrian Alpine Club, the British Mountaineering Council or by applying to:

West Mercia Insurance Services
High Street
Wombourne
WOLVERHAMPTON WV5 9DH

LANGUAGE

The language spoken throughout the region is German, though basic English is widely understood in most of the huts.

Mountain terminology

Tal	valley
Gletcher, Ferner	glacier
Eis	ice
Bach	river, stream
See lake,	tarn
Alm	alpine hut
Weg	way, footpath
Berg	mountain
Band, Grat	ledge, ridge
Nadel	needle, pinnacle
Gipfel, Spitze	summit
Wilde	snow-covered peak
Aperer	rock peak
Joch, Scharte, Sattel, Neider	col, saddle, pass
Nord, Sud, Ost, West	north, south, east, west
Links, recht,geradeaus	left, right, straight ahead
Über, unter	under, over
Wetter	weather
Regen, Sturm, Schnee,Schneien	rain, storm, snow, snowing
Schwierig	difficult
Gefährlich	dangerous
Steinslag	stone fall
Kessel	couloir
Alpenvereins	alpine club
Bergführer	professional mountain guide
Bergrettung	mountain rescue
Kabel	rope
Bett, Matratzenlager	bed, dormitory

Useful words and phrases

Ja	yes
Nein	no
Bitte	please

Danke	thank you
Auf	on
Gross, klein	large, small
Heiss, kalt	hot, cold
Alt, neu	old, new
Frei	free, vacant
Besetzt	occupied, engaged
Gut, schlecht	good, bad
Speisekarte	menu
Duschen	shower
Toiletten	toilet
Eingang	entrance
Ausgant	exit
Ankunft	arrivals
Abfahrt	departures
Bahnhof	railway station
Bushaltestelle	bus stop
Briefmarken	postage stamps
Wieviel	how much
Wo ist	where is
Wie bitte	excuse me/please repeat

Sprechen sie English?	Do you speak English?
Sprechen sie langsamer bitte	Speak slowly please
Schreiben sie es bitte auf	Please write it down
Ich verstehe niche	I don't understand
Wo ist die nachtse Bank/ Wechselstube?	Where is the nearest bank/money exchange?
Eine Einfache/Rückfahrkarte	One way/return ticket
Briefmarken für England bitte	Stamps for England please
Iche heisse	my name is
Kann ich habe	can I have
Haben sie	have you
Ich hatte gern	I'd like
Guten morgen/tag/abend	good morning/day/evening
Was kostet dans?	How much is that?
Ich möche gern zahlen	I'd like to pay
Wo ist die?	Where is the?

Camping Platz	campsite
Zelten verboten	camping forbidden
Ich bin krank	I am ill
Wie spät ist es?	What time is it?

Remember that time is recorded using the twenty-four-hour clock, particularly for bus and train timetables.

In the huts breakfast *(Frühstück)* is usually *halb sechs* or *halb sieben* and this refers to the half hour before the hour, not as it translates. Therefore *halb sechs* is not 0630 but 0530 and *halb sieben* is 06.30 not 0730.

HUTS: DESCRIPTION AND LOCATIONS

page

Amberger Hut 27

Becherhaus 27

Bremer Hut 28

Dresdner Hut 28

Franz Senn Hut...30

Hildesheimer Hut 32

Hoch Stubai Hut...34

Innsbrucker Hut 34

Müller Hut 35

Neue Regensberger Hut...36

Nürnberger Hut 36

Siegerland Hut..38

Starkenberger Hut 38

Sulzenau Hut 39

Abbreviations:

B	Beds
M	Matratzenlager
N	Nottlager

Amberger Hut

An old hut (1888), fully refurbished in 1938 and again in 1978, it stands on a rocky platform, just above the raging river of the Fischbach at the foot of the Neiderer Sulzkogal where the valley In der Sulze opens up.

Its location and height is such that it does not enjoy panoramic views of any of the local peaks since it is generally hemmed in. However, the hut is pleasant and comfortable, and it does have popular additions to the menu which are not available at other huts, namely ice-cream and *pomme frites.*

It is also one of the few huts where hot water is available throughout the day.

Owner:	DAV Amberg Section
Altitude:	2135m
Open:	1 July to early October
Facilities:	16B, 65M, 25N. Excellent toilet and restaurant facilities
Valley connections:	To Gries in Sulztal, post bus to Langenfeld
Hut connections:	Franz Senn 6-7hrs, Hoch Stubai 4-5hrs.

Becherhaus - Rifugio Regina Elena

The history of the Becherhaus is very similar to the Müller Hut which was also forfeited to Italy after World War I.

The hut was first established by D. & J.Pfurtscheller with Prof Langbein in 1886, and extended in 1900 and in 1910 to its present size. It was formerly the highest in the Stubai, being 22m higher than the Hoch Stubai Hut 3173m.

The Italians renamed the hut Rifugio Regina Elena after Queen Elena.

Owner:	CAI Verona Section
Altitude:	3195m
Location:	Wilder Freiger's S ridge
Open:	From July to September
Facilities:	24B, 40M. Good restaurant facilities, but obviously because of its height and location not as

comprehensive as other huts. Toilet facilites
are very basic due to limited water supply.

Valley connections:	None
Hut connections:	Müller 1hr, Sulzenau 5hrs, Nürnberger 3hrs.

Bremer Hut

The Bremer is an old hut 1897, which evokes much feeling placed as
it is in a true mountain situation close to the Simming glacier and
north faces of the Schneespitze and Pflerscher Hochjoch.

The hut is clad in cedar shingles, with the roof lashed down at
each corner as a reminder that the original roof was lost in a fierce
storm in the early sixties. The creeking of timbers and warmth of the
gas lighting all add to mountain environment at its best.

Owner:	DAV Bremen Section
Altitude:	2413m
Location:	On the Mitteregg Plateau above the Gschnitztal valley
Open:	Mid-June to end of September
Facilities:	23B, 35M, 6N. Moderate toilet and restaurant facilities
Valley connections:	To Gschnitztal via post bus to Feuerstein
Hut connections:	Innsbrucker 6hrs, Nürnberger 3hrs

Dresdner Hut

The location of a very old hut 1875, subsequently enlarged in 1926
then again in 1968 into its present size.

The hut is managed by Erich Hofer, a professional guide whose
family have been custodians of the hut since the turn of the century.
Photographs on the wall of the *alte Gaststube* bear witness to the
early development of the hut proudly displaying prominent
members of the Dresden Section of the German Alpine Club. The
alte Gaststube retains much of its original timber panelling together
with plaques and other mementos of a bygone age, all in stark
contrast to the newer parts of the dining room.

Dresdner Hut with the Grosser Trögler on the skyline

Sadly, with the construction of the cable-car and ski-tow facilities across the Daunkogel and Schaufel glaciers purely for the benefit of summer skiers, much of the Dresdner Hut's close environment has been somewhat spoiled and sacrificed. This, along with extensive development below the hut, means walkers will have to mingle with the many day trippers brought in from Innsbruck and other tourist resorts.

Fortunately once the sun has gone down and the clatter of machinery has stopped, the hut reverts to its true role to provide mountaineers and other mountain-lovers with simple accommodation. This it continues to do very well but it can never recapture the charisma it enjoyed in the early sixties. A popular hut, but for the wrong reasons, with a good view of the Schaufelspitze.

Owner:	DAV Dresden Section
Altitude:	2302m
Location:	At the head of the main Stubai valley below the Schaufelspitze
Open:	From mid-June to early October
Facilities:	70B, 130M. Good toilet facilites with showers available at a nominal fee. Excellent self-service restaurant facilities with the additional little extras not found on other hut menus, *pomme frites,* ice-cream, fruit salad.
Valley connections:	Mutterbergalm in the Stubaital
Hut connections:	Sulzenau 3-4hrs, Neue Regensberger 6-8hrs.

Franz Senn Hut

Perhaps the première of all the Stubai huts because of its close links with the history of the Austrian Alpine Club and its founder member after whom it is named. A portrait of Franz Senn can be found in the dining room.

Built originally in 1883 and subsequently enlarged in 1932 and 1962 to its present four-storey status, the hut is strategically placed for climbing peaks of the Alpeiner area high above the Oberberg valley. The Ruderhofspitze, Schrankogel and Lisenser Fernerkogel are all regularly climbed from the hut.

Franz Senn Hut

The hut is equally popular with day trippers because of the fairly easy access by jeep service from Milders to the Oberiss Hut. Similarly the hut is popular for DAV/ÖAV climbing courses and other aspirant alpinists. Because of the hut's popularity, sometimes it is a little crowded, but it is a big hut and everyone seems to fit in to enjoy their stay.

There is much history surrounding the hut, but most of its original internal architecture, other than the dining room, seems to have been lost at some time during refurbishment. It is a fine hut with excellent views towards the Kalkkogel and peaks of the Alpeiner.

Owner:	ÖAV Innsbruck Section
Altitude:	2147m
Location:	On a plateau at the head of the Oberberg valley below the Ruderhofspitze
Open:	From June to October
Facilities:	84B, 176M. Good restaurant and toilet facilities including hot showers
Valley connections:	To Neustift via Oberiss Hut
Hut connections:	Neue Regensberger 4hrs, Starkenberger 6-7hrs, Amberger 6-7hrs, Potsdamer 6hrs.

Hildesheimer Hut

A fine hut and one of the highest in the region (2899m). This solid three-storey stone building is ideally placed for adjacent peaks particularly the Stubai's highest peak, the Zuckerhütl (3505m).

Not surprisingly most people staying at the hut will have in mind an ascent of the mountain or its neighbouring peaks, Pfaffenschneide and Wilder Pfaff. This means that the hut is always busy and at weekends may be full.

The dining room is very pleasant and retains much of the original timber panelling from the 1937 refurbishment. The hut, as expected, is well run with a lot of effort being put into maintaining its *Gemütlichkeit*.

Standing at the hut's front door, visitors are quickly reminded that this is a high hut by a spectacular view of the ice-fall off the

Peaks of the Tribulaun from the Innsbrucker Hut
Negotiating the summit rocks on the Habicht

At the Police Hut on the Simmingjoch en route to the Nürnburger Hut

A family with youngsters (age 5 and 7) crossing the Neiderl

Hildesheimer Hut

Pfaffenschneide's Pfaffen glacier.

Owner:	DAV Hildesheim Section
Altitude:	2899m
Location:	On a rock platform above the junction of the Gaisskar and Pfaffen glacier, south of the Schaufelspitze
Open:	From early July to end September
Facilities:	24B, 56M, 25N. Good toilet and restaurant facilities
Valley connections:	To Gaisstal then to Sölden in the Ötztal valley
Hut connections:	Hoch Stubai 4hrs, Dresdner 4hrs, Siegerland 3hrs, Müller 6hrs.

Hoch Stubai Hut

The highest hut in the Stubai and the third highest hut in Austria, it was built in the early thirties to allow climbers to explore the mountains of the Daunkogel, and to provide a base midway between the Amberger and Hildesheimer huts.

A large hut for its location, it is superbly situated on a rocky knoll overlooking the Ötztal and peaks of the Daunkogel, Stubai Wildspitze, and Schaufelspitze, together with their attendant glaciers.

Not surprisingly the views from the hut are magnificent.

Owner:	DAV Dresden Section
Altitude:	3173m
Location:	On the Wildkarspitze on the edge of Wütenkar glacier
Open:	From early July to mid-September
Facilities:	10B, 37M, 6N. Good restaurant facilities but obviously because of its height not as comprehensive as other huts. Toilet facilities are moderate with very limited washing facilities due to scarce water resources.
Valley connections:	To Sölden in the Ötztal
Hut connections:	Hildesheimer 4hrs, Amberger 4hrs, Dresdner 4hrs.

Innsbrucker Hut

This superbly sited hut was fully refurbished in 1982.

Because of its proximity to the Habicht (3277m) and its relatively easy access from Innsbruck via the Pinnistal, the hut is very popular as a weekend venue - when it is often packed to capacity.

It is a charming hut with unrivalled views of the Tribulaun mountains and pinnacles of the Serleskamm.

Owner:	ÖAV Tourist Club, Innsbruck
Altitude:	2369m
Location:	On the Pinnisjoch at the foot of the Habicht's E ridge.

Open:	From late June to end September
Facilities:	40B, 120M. Excellent toilet and restaurant facilities
Valley connections:	Neustift in the Stubaital and Gschnitz
Hut connections:	Bremer 6hrs.

Müller Hut - Rifugio Cima Libera

Karl Von Müller first established a hut here in 1909. Thereafter the hut was sadly neglected over many years, since the Müller was one of those huts forfeited to Italy after World War I.

Since the hut sits on the Austro-Italian border it was generally closed to alpinists between 1926-1973 as a result of political tit-for-tat and spite going on between the two countries. During the years of instability Italian border police and the military frequently used the hut from which they could patrol the border.

Not surprisingly over this long period the hut was misused and bit by bit it fell into a ruinous state. In the early seventies the CAI made efforts to patch up the old hut using materials scavenged from its interior or from its close neighbour the Becherhaus which had fallen into a similar derelict state.

Fortunately both huts have now been re-built and re-opened. In the case of the Müller Hut, re-built means having been patched up from a derelict state using old doors and timbers. Consequently the hut is very much a ramshackle building full of creeking and groaning timbers, but it has a character not found in other huts.

At best the hut is functional and perhaps a poignant reminder of what all other huts would have been like not so many years ago, before the advent of electricity, showers and flush toilets.

But more importantly from the alpinists point of view, the hut is located in a prominent position set as it is amid the Stubai's highest mountains and its biggest glaciers. Therefore for mountaineering purposes the hut is ideally placed for excursions along the Frontier ridge. Whilst the hut is a bit basic, the views from its terrace are probably the best there are. Perhaps there is a certain amount of *Gemütlichkeit* in the old building after all!

Owner:	CAI Bolzano Section
Altitude:	3148m
Location:	At the foot of the Wilder Freigers SW ridge a little above the Pfaffenneider
Open:	From July to September
Facilities:	30B, 45M. Good restaurant facilities, but obviously because of its height and location not as comprehensive as other huts. Toilet facilities are very basic due to limited water supply.
Valley connections:	None
Hut connections:	Becherhaus 1hr, Sulzenau 4hrs, Nürnberger 4-5hrs.

Neue Regensberger Hut

A fairly modern hut built in 1931 and subsequently enlarged in 1967/8. The hut was built to replace the original hut which was forfeited to Italy after World War I. The original hut is sited in the Geisler region of the Dolomites, to the north of the Langkofel group (Sasso Piato).

Reputed to be the cleanest of all huts in the Stubai, it is a very pleasant hut, with a good view of the Habicht and Ruderhofspitze.

Owner:	DAV Regensberg Section
Altitude:	2286m
Location:	On the marshy plateau in the Falbesoner valley, below the Ruderhofspitze
Open:	From mid-June to end September
Facilities:	26B, 70M, 5N. Excellent restaurant and toilet facilities including showers
Valley connections:	To Falbesoner in the Stubaital
Hut connections:	Dresdner 6-8hrs, Franz Senn 4hrs.

Nürnberger Hut

This magnificent old hut, four stories high, is more like a hotel for tourists than a hut for mountain climbers. But its size does not detract from its obvious popularity and charm. The hut was built in

1886 and then extended in 1898 and 1908 into its present size. General refurbishment took place in 1962.

The hut has a lot of history and like a number of other huts owned by the DAV reflects the great wealth of the German Alpine Club prior to World War I. Many of the bedrooms have basins fitted with hot and cold water and a number of unique water fountains are placed along its corridors with an absolutely magnificent fountain in the dining room.

The dining room is very much *gemütlich* and pleasant with some fine carpentry details embracing its panelled walls. Not surprisingly, the hut is very popular due to its close proximity to the Wilder Freiger and the summits of the Feuerstein. This popularity has been greatly enhanced by the excellent service rendered by the Siller family who have managed the hut for well over twenty years.

The hut has a splendid view of the Feuerstein and its hanging glacier.

Neue Regensberger Hut

Owner:	DAV Nürnberg Section
Altitude:	2297m
Location:	At the head of the Langtal valley
Open:	From mid-June to October
Facilities:	57B, 84M, 10N. Excellent toilet and restaurant facilities
Valley connections:	Ranalt in the main Stubai valley
Hut connections:	Bremer 4hrs, Sulzenau: via the Niederl 3hrs, or via the Maierspitze 4 hrs.

Siegerland Hut

This is a fine stone building with large circular buttresses and a commanding view of the Ötztal.

The hut was built in 1930 and has remained unchanged since then. Its dining room is particularly warm, pleasant and *gemütlich*. Most visitors will relish sitting in its bay window enjoying a meal and a superb view of the Ötztal. It is one of the most charming huts in the Stubai.

It is also a very popular hut with the UK section of the ÖAV, so much so that the Basic Rock & Ice course is often based here for a number of days.

Owner:	DAV Siegerland Section
Altitude:	2710m
Location:	At the foot of the Sonklarspitze SW spur on a rocky platform overlooking the Windach valley
Open:	From early July to end September
Facilities:	26B, 37M, 9N. Good toilet and restaurant facilities
Valley connections:	To Gaisstal then to Sölden in the Ötztal
Hut connections:	Hildesheimer 3hrs, Müller 5hrs.

Starkenberger Hut

A tiny hut was first built here in 1900 to explore the limestone peaks of the Kalkkogel. Thereafter the hut has been regularly enlarged 1905, 1914, 1965, 1975 and 1981 - to reach its present state.

The hut is extremely popular with day visitors from Neustif͡t, who are prepared to sweat 1300m of ascent to reach it. This means that the hut is likely to be packed on arrival, but it is not unusual to have the run of the place once the sun has gone down. If you are lucky with the weather, the sunset and night sky from the hut is truly memorable.

The Starkenberger is a friendly hut whose guardian Herr Hofer will often be seen fussing over his UK visitors to ensure they have as pleasant a stay as possible. That is *gemütlich*.

Owner:	DAV Starkenberger Section
Altitude:	2229m
Location:	On the hillside above Neustift at the foot of the Hoher Bergstall
Open:	From June to October
Facilities:	13B, 41M, 10N. Excellent toilet and restaurant facilities
Valley connections:	Neustift
Hut connections:	Franz Senn 6-7hrs, Adolf Pichler 2hrs.

Sulzenau Hut

This entirely new hut was rebuilt in 1976/78 to replace the original hut which was completely demolished by an avalanche off the Sulzenaukogel in 1975. Splendid pictures in the dining room lay testimony to the awesome powers of nature that were unleashed on that fateful day. Whilst the hut shows off its new sign, the old hut sign is still proudly displayed on the wall in the hallway.

The Sulzenau is a popular hut, due to its proximity to the Zuckerhütl (3505m), and because of this it is frequently used for climbing courses organised by the DAV, ÖAV whose practise crags are evident en route to the Peiljoch.

The hut is managed by Leo Schöpf, a professional guide, and his family. Though portly in physique, he still manages to be something of a leading light at the local climbing school. He is also a connoisseur of schnapps and dining room entertainment. This is a popular hut with a fine view across the Stubaital towards the Kalkkogel and Starkenberger Hut.

Owner:	DAV Leipzig Munich Section
Altitude:	2191m
Location:	Below the snout to the Sulzenau glacier, above Grabaalm in the Stubaital
Open:	From mid-June to the end September
Facilities:	28B, 122M. Excellent toilet and restaurant facilities
Valley connections:	Grabaalm in the Stubaital
Hut connections:	Nürnberger 3-4hrs, Dresdner: via Peiljoch 3hrs, or via Grosser Trögler 4hrs.

Sulzenau Hut

Stubai Rucksack Route

Starkenberger Ht

Neder

Neustift

Oberbergtal

Lisenser
Fernerkogel

Oberisshutte

Franz Senn Ht

Stubaital

Pinnistal

Rinnensee

Pinnisalm

Schrimmenneider

Neue Regensberger Ht

Habicht

Ruderhof Sp

Pinnisjoch

Grawagrubenneider

Innsbrucker Ht

Ranalt

Mutterbergsee

Besuchalm

Mutterbergalm

Sulzenau Ht

Niederl

Nürnberger Ht

Trögler

Dresdner Ht

Bremer Ht

Peiljoch

Grunau
See

Simmingjochl

Schaufel Sp

Wilder Freiger

Wilder Pfaff

Zuckerhütl

Feuerstein

Sonklar Sp

STUBAI RUCKSACK ROUTE

GENERAL INTRODUCTION

The central Stubai Alps are served by a total of fourteen huts, providing an unlimited combination of hut to hut walks. Specifically, it is possible to link eight huts together to form the Stubai Rucksack Route, the complete traverse of which is possible without having to cross glaciers or difficult mountain passes. This makes the route ideal for mountain walkers, families and others with limited alpine experience. However, that is not to say that you will not encounter snow, steep ground or the odd scramble here and there. Also recommended are several mountains which are attainable along the route for those with sufficient experience.

The route starts at Neder, a small village a few miles before Neustift and goes first to the Innsbrucker Hut then to each of the following huts in turn: Bremer, Nürnberger, Sulzenau, Dresdner, Neue Regensberger, Franz Senn, Starkenberger, and back to end at Neustift. Apart from the Bremer Hut, each hut connects with the main Stubai valley making it possible to connect or finish the route according to your preference.

The length of the tour is 120km and ascends just over 8000m.

The route can be done in any direction though the clockwise direction as described is seen as being marginally easier.

Altitudes

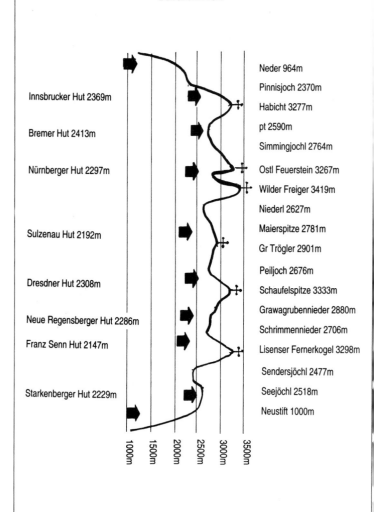

Innsbrucker Hut 2369m

Bremer Hut 2413m

Nürnberger Hut 2297m

Sulzenau Hut 2192m

Dresdner Hut 2308m

Neue Regensberger Hut 2286m

Franz Senn Hut 2147m

Starkenberger Hut 2229m

Neder 964m

Pinnisjoch 2370m

Habicht 3277m

pt 2590m

Simmingjochl 2764m

Ostl Feuerstein 3267m

Wilder Freiger 3419m

Niederl 2627m

Maierspitze 2781m

Gr Trögler 2901m

Peiljoch 2676m

Schaufelspitze 3333m

Grawagrubennieder 2880m

Schrimmennieder 2706m

Lisenser Fernerkogel 3298m

Sendersjöchl 2477m

Seejöchl 2518m

Neustift 1000m

1000m 1500m 2000m 2500m 3000m 3500m

ROUTE SUMMARY

1. Innsbruck to Neder 46
2. Neder to the Innsbrucker Hut 46
3. Excursions from the Innsbrucker Hut: 48
  3a. Ascent of the Habicht 48
  3b. Ascent of the Kalkwand 50
4. Innsbrucker Hut to the Bremer Hut....................................50
5. Bremer Hut to the Nürnberger Hut, including ascent of the Ostl Feuerstein 53
6. Nürnberger Hut to the Sulzenau Hut 56
  6a. via the Niederl 56
  6b. via the Maierspitze...59
  6c. via the Wilder Freiger 60
7. Sulzenau Hut to the Dresdner Hut: 64
  7a. via the Peiljoch 64
  7b. via the Grosser Trögler 67
8. Excursions from the Dresdner Hut. Ascent of the Schaufelspitze 69
9. Dresdner Hut to the Neue Regensberger Hut...................72
10. Neue Regensberger Hut to the Franz Senn Hut 77
11. Excursion from the Franz Senn Hut: 80
  11a. Ascent to the Rinnensee 80
  11b. Ascent of the Sommerwand 80
  11c. Ascent of the Lisenser Fernerkogel 80
12. Franz Senn Hut to the Starkenberger Hut 84
13. Excursions from the Starkenberger Hut. 87
  13a Höher Bergstall...87
14. Starkenberger Hut to Neustift 87

ROUTE DESCRIPTIONS AND SKETCH MAPS

1: Innsbruck to the Innsbrucker Hut via the village of Neder in the Stubaital

Innsbruck to Neder

From Innsbruck there is a regular bus service up the Stubai valley from the bus station adjacent to the main railway station (Hauptbahnof). Signs clearly indicate Stubaital on the bus and at the bus stop. However, if you have difficulty, there is a tourist information bureau just inside the railway station.

The journey to Neder is a pleasant ride of about an hour and includes crossing the Europa Bridge en route to the Italian border on the Brenner Pass. As you approach Neder familiarise yourself with the style of road signs which tell you the name of each village. On approach, the sign will just state the name of the village. As you leave the village a similar sign with a red stripe across it tells you that you have now left that village.

The following bus timetable has remained unchanged for the past ten years.

Innsbruck to Neustift
0750/0830/0945 then every hour up to 1700

Neustift to Innsbruck
0725 then every hour

2: Neder to the Innsbrucker Hut (2369m)

Standard time:	5 hours
Distance:	10km
Ascent:	1405m

From the bridge at Neder, a hut signpost will be found across the road pointing the way up the Pinnistal.

This single track road goes as far as Pinnisalm (6km). If you are early enjoy the walk and get into the feel of things. However, if you are late there is a jeep-cum-bus service up to Pinnisalm, which will halve the journey. There is a jeep stop in Neder across the road from

Neder to the Innsbrucker Hut

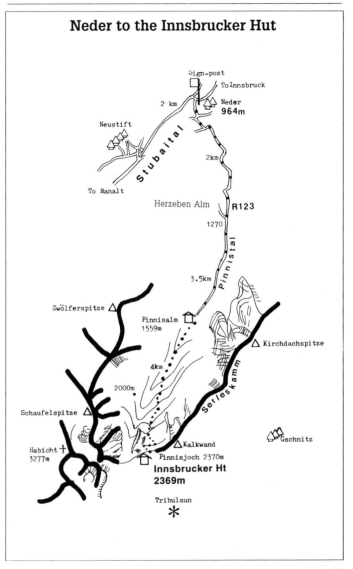

the bus stop and another one at Herzeben Alm.

After about 3km from Neder at Herzeben Alm the Pinnistal valley opens up to reveal the towering spires of the Serleskamm which provides some interesting scenery, particularly so for aspirant rock climbers, with the very impressive rock walls of the Kirchdachspitze.

Approaching Pinnisalm and beyond, the north-easterly slopes of the Habicht 3277m will dominate your viewpoint right up to the Pinnisjoch, on which, just out of sight, sits the Innsbrucker Hut.

Whatever you do, do not stay too long at the popular tourist spot at Pinnisalm (2hrs), better to take your refreshments at the hut, which has unrivalled views of the Tribulaun mountains. Beyond Pinnisalm the path quickly steepens, first gradually, then more abruptly, with 600m gained over 5km, the last 200m being zigzags up to Pinnisjoch and the hut (3hrs).

High points
A fine walk and an appropriate introduction to the Rucksack Route. The scenery is particularly good, but perhaps more akin to the Dolomites than the snow-covered peaks of the Stubai. The towering spires of the Serleskamm and Tribulaun cannot fail to impress.

Cautionary notes
The route presents no difficulty, other than it is quite a long day with a lot of uphill. Walkers need to be mindful of this and to be on their way early.

3: Excursions from the Innsbrucker Hut

3a: Ascent of the Habicht (3277m)

Standard time:	3 hours
Distance:	1¹/₂km
Ascent:	908m

This superb mountain is the highest in the eastern Stubai and was first climbed in 1836. The Habicht is best seen from the Bremer and

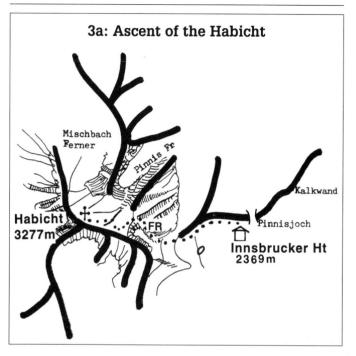

3a: Ascent of the Habicht

Mischbach Ferner

Pinnis Fr

Kalkwand

Habicht 3277m

FR

Pinnisjoch

Innsbrucker Ht 2369m

Starkenberger huts, the latter having a good view of the north face and Mischbach glacier, which is the hardest route on the mountain and one of the premier ice climbs in the Tyrol.

The ordinary route via the eastern flank is a popular outing from the Innsbrucker Hut, therefore, not surprisingly, in summer the route up the mountain is a well beaten trail.

From Pinnisjoch the Habicht signposts point out the start of the route, first heading WSW to the foot of the SE ridge. Climb this following the red waymarks: good scrambling over broken slabs aided by fixed wire ropes on the steeper section. The ridge finally emerges on a broad col at the edge of the Habicht glacier.Cross the glacier W, scramble up shattered loose rocks, moving slightly SW to gain the summit ridge, more fixed ropes, then easy ground to the large summit cross.

High points
Excellent views in all direction from the summit, particularly the main peaks of the central Stubai Alps, Tribulaun and Serleskamm plus distant peaks in the Dolomites, Zillertal and Ötztal. Sharp eyes should be able to locate the Starkenberger Hut.

Cautionary notes
Whilst the route is not technically difficult, it does call for reasonable scrambling skills on the steeper rock sections and when using fixed ropes. Because the route is well frequented, some rocks are now quite polished and this can be a problem if it is wet.

In good weather route finding is not a problem, but in mist be careful particularly in descent. Make sure to descend the Habicht glacier due east, re-tracing as far as is practicable ones own footsteps, do not go NE as the glacier ends in a sudden drop.

3b: Ascent of the Kalkwand (2564m)

A short excursion from the Innsbrucker Hut to the highest peak at the southern end of the Serleskamm. From the Pinnisjoch a small track leads NE to the summit. About 1 hour.

4: Innsbrucker Hut to the Bremer Hut

Standard time:	6 hours
Distance:	9km
Ascent:	Lots of up and down

Picking up the track from behind the hut - the route R124 contours the hillside SW to an obvious col 2559m with a large cairn on a spur on the Alfeirkamm, above a tiny lake. Excellent view of the Serleskamm-Kirchdachspitze. The col is clearly visible from the hut and the approach is frequently snow-covered.

From the col, the route continues to traverse the hillsides SW above the Pfannalm and Glättealm on or around the 2500m contour to a saddle 2511m at the foot of the Grosser Glättespitze SE ridge, west of a rock outcrop Pramarnspitze (2^1/$_2$-3hrs).

The path descends steeply W, fixed ropes, into a broad couloir

Innsbrucker Hut to the Bremer Hut

Innsbrucker Ht
2369m

Habicht ✝

2559m
R124

Glatte Alm

2749m

2511m

F R

Gschnitztal

2590m

FR

Simmingsee

Lauterersee
2425m

Wetterspitze   FR

Bremer Ht
2413m

Simmingerferner

△ Schneespitze

51

of the Beilgrube above Traulalm. Ascend rocky slopes S, across the Ochsenkogels E ridge contouring W along the 2200m contour into the boulder-strewn Traul Alm to a stream at Plattental 2400m.

Ascend broken rocky ground S to an obvious col 2590m on the E ridge of the Aussere Wetter Spitze (4hrs). The slope just before the top of the col is often snow-covered and will require a little extra care to climb. Once on top of the col, the Bremer Hut is clearly visible across the Simminger Alm with its little sea! From the col descend steep rocks, protected by fixed ropes, first SE then SSW to the foot of the ridge on the northern slopes of the Simminger Alm. Cross the Simminger Alm basin SW to the Lauterersee 2425m. Continue S to the foot of the Innere Wetter Spitze east ridge. Ascend broken rocks, good scrambling with fixed ropes to emerge on the broad plateau just below the hut (6hrs).

High points
This is a wonderful walk that is characterised by lots of up and down and plenty of challenge and ever changing scenery.

Throughout the day the scenery embraces some of the finest of the Stubai Rucksack Route. On leaving the hut, the unrivalled views of the Tribulaun peaks continue to dominate the horizon until the first col is reached on Alfeirkamm, where there is a particularly good view of the Innsbrucker Hut and the pinnacles of the Serleskamm.

By the time the Pramarnspitze is reached the magic of the Tribulaun will have given way to the snow-capped peaks of the Feuerstein and Pflerscher Hochjoch and a fabulous view of the Gschnitztal valley. The day is superbly rounded off by ending at the magnificently sited Bremer Hut.

Cautionary notes
Whilst the standard time for the route is 6 hours many parties take around 7 hours. If you have children with you, you should allow all day. Whatever your circumstance you are advised to be on your way by 7am.

Whilst the route is very much an up and down of a walk all the steep down parts tend to be protected by fixed wire ropes. The path descending from Pramarnspitze is on the scrappy side due to a combination of poor ground and lack of maintenance. Because the route crosses a number of ridges and spurs, patches of old snow tend to linger on the north-facing slopes and in gullies, in particular north of the Alfeirkamm opposite the Innsbrucker Hut and on the northern side of the col when crossing the Äussere Wetter Spitze. Neither are insurmountable but they can be problematic. Whilst the route is adequately waymarked, it is best avoided in bad weather.

5: Bremer Hut to the Nürnberger Hut

Standard time:	3 hours
	6 hours with an ascent of the Feuerstein
Distance:	5km
Ascent:	351m to the Simmingjoch
	1254m to the Ostl Feuerstein

From the hut proceed W along the obvious path, R102. The path rises steadily across grass and rocky slopes amid fine scenery until just below Simmingjochl 2764m when it rises steeply, aided by fixed ropes to the col and the tiny hut used by the border police (1hr). Excellent view of the Feuerstein and Wilder Freiger.

From the col descend steep rocks N, aided by fixed wire ropes to the head of a couloir, frequently snow-covered, below the Innere Wetter Spitze. Proceed W down scree slopes along a reasonably marked path into the upper basin of the Grübl cirque, characterised by its glacial debris of strewn boulders and where many streams congregate, point 2420m (2hrs). From hereabouts the Nürnberger Hut and Wilder Freiger are clearly visible. Continue to follow the obvious path descending first SW, then NW, then SW over broken ground and some steep rock sections with fixed cables to the raging torrents of the Langtal river coming from the Grübl glacier. Cross the planks that form the bridge and proceed in a NW direction, scrambling up and over slabby rocks to the very substantial four-storey Nürnberger Hut (3hrs).

High points
A splendid day full of scenic interest, particularly of the north faces

Bremer Hut to the Nürnberger Hut

of the Pflerscher Hochjoch and Feuerstein. The view from the Simmingjochl of the Wilder Freiger is particularly good, from where it is not unusual to see the dawn patrol crossing the upper snow slopes of the Freiger glacier on their way up the mountain.

Cautionary notes
Generally the route is quite straightforward and well marked. However, the fixed rope sections and the couloir on the north side of the Simmingjochl can prove difficult to negotiate when snow-covered as is frequently the case early in season. In such circumstances members of the party are advised to stay close to each other.

Ascent of the Ostlicher Feuerstein 3267m from the Simmingjochl

From the police hut, where parties may leave rucksacks, head off S along the ridge to gain the Aperer Feuerstein glacier at 2749m. Proceed up the snow slope of the glacier SSW to the Nürnberger Scharte 2914m. Cross the col onto the W side of the ridge and continue up the glacier SE to below point 3026m. Contour across the glacier in a SE arc, to below the Feuerstein's NW ridge, some crevasse danger at the edges, then climb steepening snow slopes, bergschrund, to gain access to the NW ridge. Continue up the rocky ridge to the large metal summit cross (about 2-2^{1}/₂hrs).

High point

A fine route up a particularly neglected mountain. Indeed you are most likely to find that you have the mountain to yourself. Aspirant alpinists may wish to note that the steep north-facing slopes immediately below the summit provide an alternative way up the mountain, providing the group have sufficient ice screws to make a safe ascent, and the necessary skills.

Once on the summit, the mountain affords some fine views particularly of the Habicht and along the Frontier ridge into the South Tyrol. From the summit sharp eyes should be capable of locating the Becherhaus on its rocky knoll to the left of the Wilder Freiger.

Cautionary notes

Whilst crevasses are not generally a problem, the bergschrund running parallel with the NW ridge can be. In such circumstances, you may wish to try gaining access by point 3168m on the SW ridge from the Pflerscher Hochjoch, then traverse the exposed rocky ridge to the summit.

From the summit the route across to the west summit and beyond may look tempting to aspirant alpinists. However, for the purpose of these notes, the route is not recommended due to the increased difficulty and corresponding increase in exposure.

Aperer Feuerstein (2965m)

For those who feel an ascent of the Feuerstein is too difficult an undertaking the Aperer Feuerstein is a worthwhile excursion and provides first class views of the Feuerstein and across the void to the Wilder Freiger.

From the police hut, head off S along the ridge to gain the Aperer Feuerstein glacier at 2749m. Proceed up the snow slope SSW to the Nürnberger Scharte 2914m.

Scramble up the obvious rock ridge NW to the summit (about 1hr). From the summit either retrace your tracks in descent, or continue along the ridge N to point 2825m. Descend steeply E down the rock to regain the remnants of the Aperer Feuerstein glacier and on back to the police hut.

6: Nürnberger Hut to the Sulzenau Hut

There is a choice of three routes to the Sulzenau Hut and these are described in order of difficulty.

6a: The Niederl (2627m)

Standard time:	3 hours
Distance:	4km
Ascent:	347m

From the hut proceed W, R102, along the Central Alpine Way to a signpost pointing the way to the Maierspitze.

Continue W, up and over rocky slabs in a series of zigzag-type staircases, first gradually then steeply at the top, fixed ropes, to the Niederl 2627m an obvious col with a large wooden cross on the ridge connecting the Urfallspitze with the Maierspitze (1hr). Excellent views in all directions particularly Wilder Freiger and Feuerstein.

From the Niederl descend a very steep rock face, traversing to and fro along a series of ledges, protected by fixed ropes, to a tiny lake. Good picnic site. Continue W along a good path to its junction with the path from the Maierspitze.

Thereafter proceed SSW to the Grunausee with its spectacular view of the Wilder Freiger and its glacier system. Follow the track NW on the right bank of the Grunaubach stream to a footbridge. Cross this and head WNW over easy ground to the very modern Sulzenau (3hrs).

Nürnberger Hut to the Sulzenau Hut

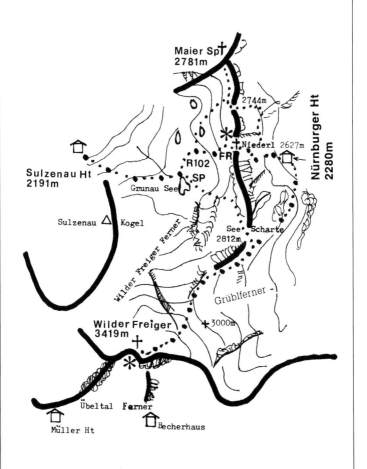

Wilder Freiger and Wilder Freiger Glacier from above Grunausee

6b: Ascent of the Maierspitze (2781m)

Standard time:	4 hours
Distance:	6km
Ascent:	501m

From the hut proceed W, R102, for a short distance to a signpost where the routes to Niederl and Maierspitze split.

Now ascend the gradually steepening rocky path, first traversing NW then N in the direction of an obvious ridge. Scramble over rocks to gain the ridge at point 2553m. Continue W, scrambling along the ridge, aided by fixed ropes on steeper sections, to a col on the Maierspitze south ridge (1^1/$_2$hrs). Excellent view.

Proceed N along the obvious ridge via point 2775m, first steeply then drop sharply for a short distance before continuing more gradually to the craggy top with its park bench seat and large summit cross (2hrs).

From the summit return to the col by the same route, then descend steep rocks SW to a small lake at 2552m on the old glacier basin of the Schafgrübl. Good picnic site. Rejoin the path from the Niederl, R102, a little further on. The route from here is as for the Niederl.

High points   Niederl-Maierspitze
Both routes are famed for their panoramic views of the Wilder Freiger. Likewise, each location provides a good vantage point for reviewing the previous day's activity, with an equally good view of the Feuerstein and the backdrops across the void to the Simmingjochl with its tiny police hut.

Thereafter, the tiny lakes above Grunausee provide ideal sites for picnics, particularly if you remembered to purchase extra tasty provisions like Apfelstrudel and filled a water bottle with beer or wine, while you sit back and enjoy the view of the Wilder Freiger mirrored on the surface.

An excellent day with some truly memorable scenery, though a little short on duration.

Cautionary notes   Niederl-Maierspitze

The only caution that is needed is in descending the very steep rock faces, more so on the west side of the Niederl. Anyone who is not entirely vertigo free should descend the rocks with a partner for a little moral support.

6c: Ascent of the Wilder Freiger (3419m)

Standard time:	4 hours (7-8 hours hut to hut)
Distance:	8km
Ascent:	1139m

An extremely popular route up a beautiful snow-capped mountain.

From the hut, signpost, move off S, over rocks on a well defined track for about 15 minutes, where the track splits, signpost.

The track heading off SE is R102 leading to the Simmingjochl and Bremer Hut. Continue S along the well defined rocky path until it turns SW up a series of zigzags below the Urfallspitze. The route continues SW along the Urfallspitze east flank and rises steadily up and over boulders before finally giving way to a gap in the ridge to the See Scharte 2740m (2hrs).

Apart from providing an excellent view, the See Scharte provides an opportunity to deposit some of the contents of rucksacks to allow a lighter ascent of the mountain to be made.

From the See Scharte continue SW over rocks and boulders passing below points 2945m and 2934m to a permanent large patch of snow south of the Gamsspitzl 3052m. Get onto the snow by descending W for a few metres. Ascend the snow in a SW arc, regaining the obvious rocky ridge around point 3065m. Scramble along the rocky ridge in a SSW direction amid spectacular glacier scenery until its end at the junction of the Wilder Freiger Ferner and Grüblferner glacier systems.

Proceed up the broad snow ridge SSW avoiding obvious crevasses to point 3313m. Now head SW over the snowfield to the Signalgipfel 3392m with its obvious disused customs building.

Continue up the snowfield NW along the edge of a rocky ridge overlooking the Übeltal glacier and South Tyrol to the summit with its large wooden cross (4hrs). Superb panoramic view.

Summit rocks of the Wilder Freiger

Routes described:
Müller Hut to the Nürnberger.
Normal route up the mountain from the Nürnberger Hut

61

In descent retrace your steps back to the See Scharte (about 1hr).

Cross the See Scharte onto the west flank of the Urfallspitze and descend the steep snow that form the remnants of the Kleiner Grunauferner glacier. Descend the glacier's right bank keeping close to the rocks, NW, until it gives way to glacial debris at its foot where the route is waymarked by the usual daubs of red paint. The Sulzenau Hut is visible from here on. The route continues NW and descends rapidly towards the Grunausee where it joins routes coming from the Niederl and Maierspitze (1hr). Good views of the icefall off the Wilder Freiger Ferner. Also keep an eye open for the Grawagrubennieder, the highest pass on the Rucksack Route which is clearly visible below the Seespitze to the NW. From Grunausee continue NW then WNW on R102, to the very modern Sulzenau Hut.

High points
A first-rate day out up a beautiful and justifiably popular mountain amid superb scenery.

Early birds should be on their way by 0600hrs to avoid the rush and enjoy the pre-dawn coolness for most of the way to the See Scharte, by which time the sun will have illuminated the twin peaks of the Feuerstein with its hanging glaciers to spectacular effect.

The See Scharte is an ideal place for a second breakfast stop and provides the first opportunity to have a look on the other side of the mountain - it is here the route opens up and provides that essential feeling of space.

Equally, because the See Scharte enjoys a fair amount of sunshine, many flowers grow in its vicinity particularly the vivid blue spring gentian and pink moss campion. Anyone who does not want to climb the mountain may find the idea of sunbathing at the See Scharte an appealing alternative to the Niederl-Maierspitze traverse whilst waiting the return of their friends from climbing the mountain.

From the See Scharte the route opens up to provide some spectacular glacier scenery, particularly so along the rocky ridge south of the Gamsspitzl.

Once on the summit, the view is perhaps the most extensive in the region for the summit is placed amid the Stubai's biggest mountains and its largest glaciers. The view into Italy across the snow-capped mountains of the South Tyrol and beyond to the Dolomites is immense with the lonely Becherhaus standing isolated in the near distance just below the summit.

The Müller Hut can be seen from the Signalgipfel.

On the west and northern horizon the whole of the Stubai's main peaks can be seen from the Zuckerhütl, Ruderhofspitze and across the main Stubai valley in a wide panoramic arc to the Habicht. On the far horizon lie the peaks of the Ötztal in the west with the Zillertal and Venediger to the east. The Dolomites lie to the south, the Karwendal and German Alps to the north.

This is an excellent day out and one to savour and remember.

Cautionary notes

Since most people staying at the Nürnberger Hut will have in mind an ascent of the Freiger, this often means that the route can be quite crowded. Because of this popularity, route finding up the mountain should present no real difficulties as it is a very well beaten trail throughout the summer months. However, whilst not a serious undertaking the Wilder Freiger is a big mountain set amongst the Stubai's largest glaciers. This means that warm air from the Italian south quickly condenses to form thick cloud making route finding across the summit snows very hazardous. The mountain frequently starts to cloud up by mid morning.

In cloudy conditions the descent from the summit should be strictly adhered to by retracing one's steps back to the Signalgipfel and Gamsspitzl. Any idea of descending direct from the summit across the Grüblferner to point 3324 by cutting across the glacier should be avoided as walkers are frequently led over easy ground into a series of big crevasses on the 3300 contour. Whilst crevasses are not normally a problem on the upper slopes, they do exist and have become more prevalent in recent years, due to minimal winters.

7: Sulzenau Hut to the Dresdner Hut

Standard time:	3 hours via the Peiljoch 2676m
	4 hours via the Grosser Trögler 2901m
Distance:	4km
Ascent:	485m via the Peiljoch
	710m via the Grosser Trögler

Leaving the conviviality of the Sulzenau Hut behind, there is a choice of routes to the Dresdner Hut.

7a: The Peiljoch (2676m)

From the hut follow R102 SW for a short distance, until the branch track to the Trögler is reached. Signpost. Proceed W, passing the branch track for the Lübecher Way on the left, R136, and the crags used by the ÖAV climbing school on the right. Continue over rocky ground W, then SW along the left-hand moraine of the Sulzenau glacier, fixed ropes in places and a wooden plank across the edge of a rocky slab. Continue SE across the flank of the Grosser Trögler until immediately below the Peiljoch and above the snout of the Sulzenau glacier at point 2580m. Signpost for the Zuckerhütl. Bear right and proceed NW up a steep path to the Peiljoch characterised by its many stone cairns (about 1¹/₂hrs). Excellent view of the Sulzenau glacier's icefall and the Wilder Pfaff.

From the col, descend rocks NW across a broad couloir, then steeply down a ridge along a staircase of rocks and boulders, exposed in places - aided by fixed ropes - until the path rejoins the route from the Grosser Trögler coming from the east. Signpost for the Dresdner Hut.

The Dresdner Hut is now clearly visible a little above the cable-car station. There is also a good view of the Schaufelspitze and the peaks of the Daunkogel. Continue to descend along the obvious path W, then NW over rocks and grassy slopes, on past the cable-car station to the very commercial Dresdner Hut (3hrs).

High points

Whilst the route may not have the scenic interest of the Grosser Trögler, it provides a suitable poor weather alternative, plus an

Above Grunau See en route to the Sulzenau Hut

Rinnensee with the Seespitze in the background

Sulzenau Hut to the Dresdner Hut

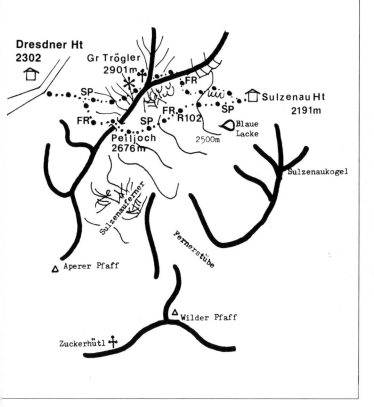

opportunity for a closer inspection of the Sulzenauferner, the glacier system and icefall.

The Peiljoch is characterised by the many stone cairns built by enthusiastic if somewhat amateur stone masons so that the col is more reminiscent of sacred ground in the mighty Himalayas than the Austrian Tyrol.

Approaching the Schrimmenieder en route to the Franz Senn Hut

Wilder Pfaff, Fernerstube and Sulzenau Glacier ice fall from the Peiljoch

Once across the Peiljoch there are some excellent views of the peaks across the Schaufel and Daunkogel glaciers including the Ruderhofspitze.

Overall, a pleasant trek, though a little short on duration. Ideal as a rest day to keep a party moving.

Cautionary notes

A straightforward route with no specific difficulties. However, in poor weather, particularly cloud, some care needs to be exercised on the fixed ropes and to keep to the correct track immediately below the Peiljoch, point 2580m. At this point a path of sorts continues SW onto the Sulzenau glacier and it is not uncommon for the right-hand turn up to the Peiljoch to be missed. Remember to bear right at the signpost for the Zuckerhütl.

7b: The Grosser Trögler (2901m)

Highly recommended with a magnificent view of the Zuckerhütl 3505m the Stubai's highest peak.

From the hut follow R102, SW, for a short distance until a branch track is reached. Signpost. R102 continues to the Dresdner Hut via the Peiljoch. From the signpost the route continues NW over grassy slopes and the broken rocks of the Hohe Salze. At point 2500m the path steepens and climbs in a series of zigzags through a rock barrier, with fixed ropes on the steeper sections, until the broad ridge north of the Kleine Trögler is reached. This small plateau is famed for its profusion of alpine flowers, particularly gentian and edelweiss. Excellent scenery in all directions from here on. Proceed SW along the ridge on a good track, rock scrambles here and there, to the summit ($2^1/2$ hrs) with its large wooden cross inscribed to the memory of Peter Trögler, a professional guide who was sadly killed in a climbing accident on the mountain many years ago.

From the summit descend steeply over rocky slabs, first SW then WNW down through a narrow couloir in a series of zigzags to its junction with the track from the Peiljoch. Follow R102, W then NW over grass and rocks to the hut ($1^1/2$ hrs).

High points

A justifiably popular route with a truly magnificent view of the

Wilder Pfaff, Zuckerhutl, Pfaffenschneid and convergence of the Ferner Stube and Sulzenau Glaciers viewed from the top of the Grosser Trögler. The Pfaffensattle is the obvious col between the Wilder Pfaff and Zuckerhutl

Zuckerhütl 3505m - the Stubai's highest mountain and its attendant glacier. It is from the Trögler's summit that the Zuckerhütl's namesake of Sugarloaf will be apparent. Equally the summit is a good place from which to recce the route to the Neue Regensberger Hut.

Cautionary notes
A straightforward route with no real difficulties other than the short section involving the fixed ropes when a little brute force will be required to climb a number of rock steps.

8: Ascent of the Schaufelspitze (3333m)

Standard time:	4 hours
Distance:	3km
Ascent:	1142m

A pleasant popular mountain nicknamed the shovel mountain because of its broad summit, dominating the head of the valley above the Dresdner Hut. Much of the route is sadly spoiled by the many ski-tow pylons dotted across the Daunkogel and Schaufel glaciers.

From the hut head off W, following R135 for a short distance until a stream is reached, with a footbridge and signpost for Eisee.

From here R135 continues to the Neue Regensberger Hut. Cross the stream continuing W through the rocky area of the Gamsgarten, ascending steadily to a large open area at the foot of the Daunkogel glacier complete with cable-car station and small lake, Eisee, to where the track forks (signpost).

The right-hand track goes to the Daunjoch and Hoch Stubai or Amberger huts. Follow the left-hand path SW over glacier debris heading for the obvious cable-car station at the foot of the Schaufel glacier.

Either a) Get onto the glacier around the 2700m contour and ascend it SW diagonally to the rock island at 3013m. Continue S up the glacier to the obvious col, the Bildstöckljoch 3133m (3hrs). Some crevasses on the 3000m contour.

b) Continue S up rocks above the Schaufel glacier's right bank, path of sorts to the cable-car station at 2850m.

Get onto the glacier and cross it SW until S of the rock island 3013m, then head S up the glacier to the Bildstöckljoch. Alternatively, from the cable-car station simply follow the row of pylons to the col.

Cross the Bildstöckljoch S, onto the upper snows of the Windach glacier to the Eisjoch 3149m. The summit is clearly visible from here. Excellent view of the Ötztal, and an unusual view of the Zuckerhütl.

From the Eisjoch turn NE, and cross the upper snows of the Gaisskar glacier to another col, the Isidorneider 3158m. Continue E, proceed over rocks and boulders, paths of sorts to the summit with its large wooden cross (4hrs).

A further alternative is to make use of the cable-car system to the Eisgrat, then to follow route (b) to the Bildstöckljoch and onto the summit (about $2^{1/2}$hrs from the hut).

Participants may wish to consider this mode of ascent as an afternoon excursion after crossing the Peiljoch/Grosser Trögler in the morning!

High points

Sadly all the main viewpoints are overshadowed by the ski-tow pylons and other man-made structures put up in the eighties to satisfy the appetites of summer skiers.

There are however, a number of places that remain relatively intact and provide uncluttered vistas. The first of these is when crossing the Daunkogel glacier around the 3000m contour looking west along the glacier to the Stubai Wildspitze. Then on the glacier plateau of the Eisjoch looking to the Ötztal, and finally once on the summit looking west to the Zuckerhütl.

Cautionary notes

A straightforward route with little to hinder one's progress. There are crevasses along the upper sections of the route, but these are easily by-passed. The only other risk comes from the summer skiers - the best advice is to keep well out of their way.

Dresdner Hut: Ascent of the Schaufelspitze

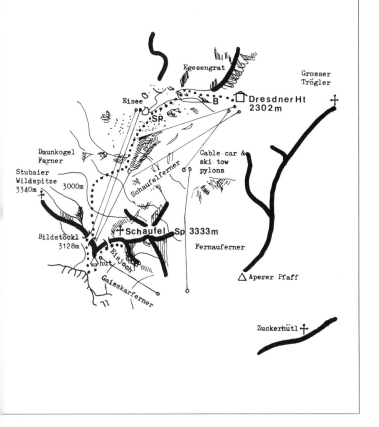

9: Dresdner Hut to the Neue Regensberger Hut

Standard time:	6 hours (This is rarely achieved, 8 hours should be allowed.)
Distance:	11km
Ascent:	A lot of up and down

A fine day's outing and one of the longest of the Stubai Rucksack Route, involving crossing the route's highest pass.

From the hut follow route R138 W, to a stream with a footbridge and its junction with the path leading to the Schaufelspitze (signpost). Keep on the left bank of the stream coming from the Gamsgarten, heading WNW over rocks to a col, signpost, on the west ridge of the Egesengrat, overlooking the Wilde Grube. The col is also home to a family of marmots - if you can proceed silently you may catch sight of this somewhat elusive furry mountain dweller if you are lucky.

Descend the scree and rocky slope N, first steeply (fixed ropes) then more gradually into the Wilde Grube, a large open area where many streams congregate, until due E of the Hint Daunkopf.

Cross the streams, the track contours around the open couloir of the Glamergrube, climbing steadily on a good path, across the steep hillside of alpine pasture until south of the Mutterberger See (signpost).

The route continues NW to the tiny lake at Hohe Grube, an ideal place for a second breakfast with probably the best view there is of the Schaufelspitze. Continue along the good path NW ascending steadily across the southern flank of the Ruderhofspitze in the direction of a col with a large stone cairn. Climb the rocks to the col (signpost). This cairn marks approximately the halfway point in the day's promenade, in addition to providing an excellent panorama across the main Stubai valley to the snow-covered peaks of the Wilder Freiger, Wilder Pfaff and Zuckerhütl. The Dresdner Hut is just about visible from here.

From the col, descend the steep rock flank and continue NE, contouring across the rocky couloir to another col on the Schafspitze 2760m. Scramble down steep rocks, fixed ropes, continuing NE across the rocky southern flank of the Gamsspitzl, in a series of rocky steps and zigzags to the Grawagrubennieder 2888m, a col on

Dresdner Hut to the Neue Regensberger Hut

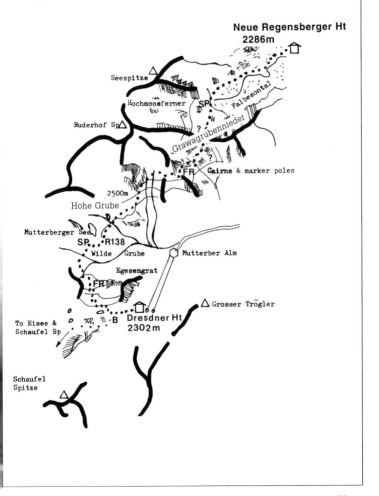

Dresdner Hut to the Neue Regensberger Hut.
Negotiating fixed ropes

the Ruderhofspitze east ridge (signpost). The route is part waymarked for a short distance before the col by marker poles.

From the col, descend steeply N over loose rocks and other dubious ground in a series of zigzags, to reach the upper edge of the Hochmoos glacier. Get onto the glacier, often made difficult because of the bergschrund, look for route markers and cairns. Cross the glacier N, then NNE, over rocky ground strewn with large boulders to the Falbesoner See (signpost).

The route now proceeds easily on a good path NE along the Falbesonertal, to the very pleasant Neue Regensberger Hut.

High points

An excellent day out full of scenic interest with the odd challenge here and there!

The first highlight of the day is the area around the Hohe Grube with its tiny lake and fine view of the Schaufelspitze. Thereafter, negotiating the high level path midway between the rocky spurs below the Gamsspitzl provides some great scenery across the Stubaital to the main snow-capped peaks along the Austrian-Italian border. Once across the Grawagrubennieder, the walk along the Falbesonertal to the very popular Neue Regensberger Hut is one of the most pleasant of the Rucksack Route with an excellent view of the Ruderhofspitze's icefall and then, a little further on, a good view of the Habicht.

Cautionary notes

Whilst the route has a liberal amount of sections making use of fixed ropes, the only real objective danger that requires more than a degree of caution is in the crossing of the Grawagrubennieder. In descent, the route is a grotty affair, being a mix of rocks, scree and other loose rubble.

At its lower edge, where the rocks approach the Hochmoos glacier, route finding is not always obvious. Parties are advised to keep close together to avoid knocking rocks down on each other and to provide assistance whilst crossing the loose rock and scree slopes. Care also needs to be exercised in getting onto the glacier, which is more often than not a mix of old snow and ice. Nevertheless, a bergschrund is often present and this can make the move onto the glacier quite difficult. Look for marker poles and the usual daubs of red paint.

Dresdner Hut to the Neue Regensberger Hut:
Approaching the Neue Regensberger Hut along the Falbesoner

Apart from the difficulty in negotiating the Grawagrubennieder's northern slopes, this section of the route is no place to be caught in bad weather.

The only other word of caution is that the route is quite long. Though 6 hours is the standard time between huts, this is rarely achieved and 7 to 8 hours is more normal, therefore you should be on your way no later than 8am.

Neue Regensberger Hut to the Franz Senn Hut

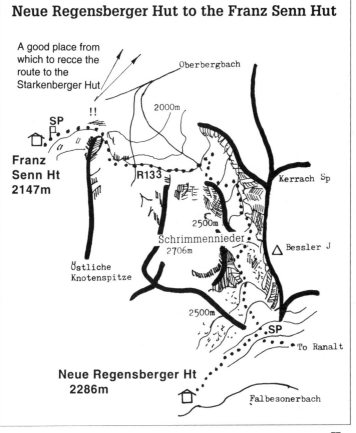

10: Neue Regensberger Hut to the Franz Senn Hut

Standard time:	4 hours
Distance:	6½km
Ascent:	420m

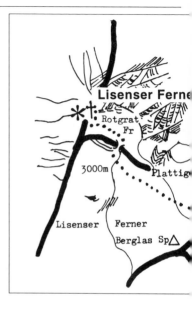

From the pleasant Neue Regensberger Hut follow R133, NE along the level path of the Windtratten to the foot of the ridge coming down from the Sommerwantl. Signpost. Turn left, NNW and ascend steep slopes, over rocks and scree, traversing the couloir in a series of long zigzags up to the broad col of the Schrimmennieder 2706m (about 2hrs). Good view down the valley to Ranalt and across the void to the Habicht.

Descend from the col NW, along a fine rocky staircase on the Dr Franz Höertnagl Weg down through the Platzengrube couloir in a wide arc until it levels out on the 2200m contour. Continue along the good track W, across the flank of the Kuhgschwez just N of the spurs, Uelasgrat and Gschwezgrat coming down from the Östliche Knotenspitze and on to the very impressive Franz Senn Hut.

High points

After the very long walk from the Dresdner to the Neue Regensberger Hut, this has to be considered as a sort of rest day.

Sadly the route is a little hemmed in and does not have any magnificent views to compare with the previous day's outings. However, the view from the Schrimmennieder down to Ranalt and the Habicht is quite spectacular. Likewise the view of the snow-capped peaks of the Alpeiner on the approach to the Franz Senn Hut can be quite impressive particularly so if the alpenrose bushes are still in flower.

Franz Senn Hut:
Ascent of the Linsenser Fernerkogel

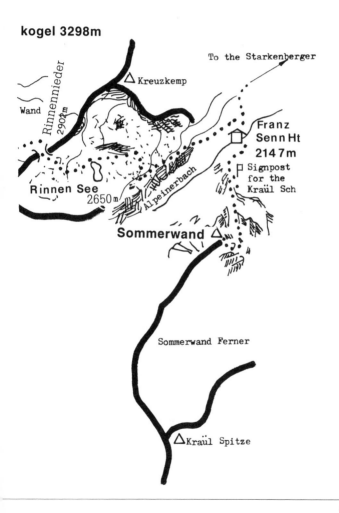

kogel 3298m

To the Starkenberger

Kreuzkemp

Rinnennieder Wand 2902m

Franz Senn Ht 2147m

Signpost for the Kraül Sch

Rinnen See 2650m

Alpeinerbach

Sommerwand

Sommerwand Ferner

Kraül Spitze

Cautionary notes
Perhaps the most straightforward day's outing of the whole of the Rucksack Route with no difficulties whatsoever.

11: Excursions from the Franz Senn Hut

11a: Rinnensee (2650m)   1¹/₂ hours

A delightful alpine lake with magnificent views of the Ruderhofspitze and Seespitze, this is an ideal picnic site with many photographic opportunities. Follow the route description for the Lisenser Fernerkogel.

11b: Sommerwand (2677m)   2 hours

A pleasant walk whose lower summit provides a good view of the Seespitze and Kraülspitze. But more specifically the Sommerwand is famed for its profusion of Alpine flowers, including the shy edelweiss, which grow on its south-facing slopes.

From the hut follow the well marked path south, signpost, over rock and grassy slopes around the foot of the Vord Sommerwands long ridge then head SW to a signpost. The path continues SW over the Sommerwand glacier to the Kraülscharte. From the signpost, turn R, N, up a series of zigzags along a rock path to the rocky terrace of the Sommerwand.

11c: Ascent of the Lisenser Fernerkogel (3298m)

Standard time:	4 hours (This is rarely achieved and 5 hours is more realistic.)
Distance:	5km
Ascent:	1151m

A fine mountain with one of the most extensive panoramic views in the Alps.

On the SW ridge of the Sonklarspitze approaching the Höhes Eis

Above: On the Sulztal Glacier approaching the Wutenkarsattel en-route to the Hoch Stubai Hut.   Below: Approaching the Muller Hut on the Obeltal Glacier. Becherhaus on the right hand ridge

From the hut, cross the Alpeinerbach stream and follow R132 for about 15 minutes up the grassy path leading to the Lisens valley and the Starkenberger Hut until it branches off left, signpost. Turn left and head SW on a good path over grass and rocky slopes ascending steadily, with zigzags in places, to the Rinnensee 2650m (about $1^{1}/_{2}$ hrs). An excellent view of the Seespitze and Ruderhofspitze group reflected on its surface make this a good place for a picnic! Continue W for a short distance then head NW up steep rocky slopes, fixed ropes, to the Rinnennieder 2902m, a small col overlooking the Lisenser glacier. The col provides good situation type scenery and an excellent vantage point to recce the route up the mountain located immediately opposite to the NW.

Descend the rocks on the W of the col to the edge of the Lisenser glacier, bergschrund. Get onto the glacier and cross it NW, crevasses, to the base of the rock barrier, the Plattigewand. Scramble up the rocks around the 3000m, contour and traverse them along a rock terrace for a short distance NE to gain the Rotgratferner glacier at point 3045m. Get onto the glacier and ascend the steep slope (right bank) NW parallel to the Rotgratspitze SE ridge, until it is possible to cross the glacier NNW above a series of crevasses to the opposite bank below the summit. Gain the rocks and scramble over boulders and slabs, loose in places, up the short south ridge to the summit with its slender metal cross (about 5hrs).

High points

A fine route up a magnificent mountain and highly recommended.

The route embraces many scenic attractions, notably the view up the Alpeiner valley with its glaciers and snow-capped peaks. Then the Rinnensee, with the peaks of the Ruderhofspitze, Seespitze, Kraülspitze, mirrored on its surface, usually provides aspirant photographers with a variety of photogenic opportunities. Equally the Rinnensee is an ideal place for a picnic or a short day excursion. It is a lovely place, and one to savour.

Beyond the Rinnensee, the Rinnennieder provides a good mountaineering situation, being isolated and a little exposed on both sides of the ridge. The col provides that essential ingredient of a little excitement, plus the first real opportunity to see the mountain and its attendant glaciers.

Main Stubai peaks looking SW from the summit of the Lisenser Fernerkogel

Crossing the glaciers and scrambling up the rocks is good wholesome mountaineering and thoroughly enjoyable. All these qualities are reinforced once the summit has been attained and as previously mentioned the view from the summit is one of the most extensive in the entire Alps, and without doubt, in the Eastern Alps.

Moreover, it is the Stubai peaks which dominate the scenery, especially the Schrankogel and around to the Zuckerhütl, Wilder Freiger, and Habicht. Beyond the Stubai on the far horizons are the Ötztal, Zillertal, South Tyrol, Dolomites, Kalkkogel and Karwendal, whilst those with sharp eyes will be able to locate the Westfalenhaus Hut nestling in the Langtal valley over 1000 metres below. If the day is blessed with clear blue skies, spend as much time as possible trying to absorb such a panoramic view for it is magnificent.

Cautionary notes
For such a fine mountain, the route has few objective dangers. However, the glaciers can be a little problematic, particularly the bergschrund below the Rinnennieder. Whilst this is usually small and can be traversed by a single jump, nevertheless, it does exist, and may vary season to season. Similarly, the crevasses on the Rotgrat glacier, which run parallel and diagonally to it, will involve some route finding skill. Thereafter, the ascent of the summit rocks along the south ridge requires a degree of care as the mid section is quite loose and the exposure on the west side of the ridge is very airy with a spectacular drop. Walkers who are not totally vertigo free are advised to keep to the bulk of the mountain.

12: Franz Senn Hut to the Starkenberger Hut

Standard time:	6 hours (This is rarely achieved and 7 hours is more realistic.)
Distance:	12km
Ascent:	A lot of up and down

The longest day's outing of the Rucksack Route, full of scenic interest and a fitting way to complete the tour.

Leaving behind the very impressive Franz Senn Hut, cross over

Franz Senn Hut to the Starkenberger Hut

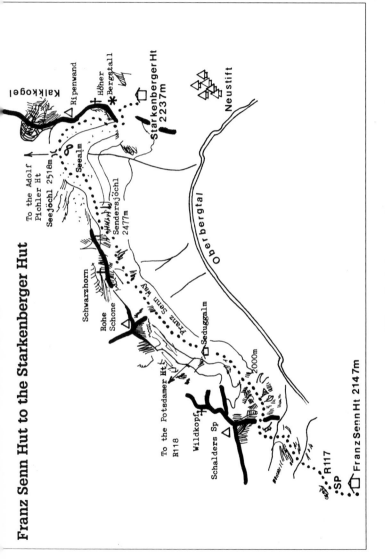

the bridge and follow R132 NW along a steep grassy path, bypassing the track leading to the Lisenser Fernerkogel until its junction with R117 where a prominent stream is crossed. R132, the left branch, continues over the Grosse Horntal into the Lisens valley.

Continue NE along the Franz Senn Weg R117, following a good path over grass and rocky slopes, crossing a number of rocky spurs on the southern flank of the Schalderspitze, excellent view back to Seduggalm 2249m. This tiny chamois hunters' hut is located a little before the halfway stage and provides an ideal opportunity for refreshments. The hut is located at the junction of R118 which leads over the Wildkopfscharte to the Potsdamer Hut. Continue NE along R117, on a good path contouring across the hillside high above the Oberberg valley on the 2300m contour, past the Schwarzhorn until it climbs steadily to the col at the Sendersjöchl 2477m. This overlooks the Senders and Fotscher valleys to the north, giving an excellent panoramic view across the whole of the Stubai.

Continue ENE along the broad ridge to the Steinkogel 2589m with its excellent view of the jagged peaks of the Kalkkogel. Descend slightly contouring over scree slopes NE to the Seejöchl 2518m (signpost) and junction with routes from the Adolf Pichler Hut.

Follow R116 SE traversing the scree slopes below the Riepenwand and Hoher Bergstall on good but slightly exposed path to the very picturesque Starkenberger Hut.

High points

A magnificent day out full of scenic interest and a fitting way to end the Stubai Rucksack Route.

Early in the day the scenery is dominated by looking back to the Franz Senn Hut, which has a memorable view of the snow-capped peaks of the Alpeiner, particularly Ruderhofspitze and Schrankogel. Once at the tiny chamois hunters' hut at Seduggalm, whose motto reads "my kingdom is a flock of white sheep and my little hut is my castle", the peaks of the Alpeiner will have eased back and merged with the whole of the Stubai. Thereafter, the jagged limestone peaks of the Kalkkogel, which are more akin to the Dolomites than the Stubai, becomes evident and announce the end of the tour.

Once at the Starkenberger Hut, the immediate scenery is dominated with a fine view of the Habicht. Perhaps, however, the most spectacular of panoramic views is when the sun has gone down, when the sunset and night sky seen from the Starkenberger Hut it truly memorable.

Cautionary notes
Despite its length, the route has no real difficulties. However, it is a good day out and walkers need to be on their way by 8am.

13 Excursions from the Starkenberger Hut

13a: Ascent of the Hoher Bergstall (2611m)

A short excursion of about 1 hour. From the hut follow R115, N up steep scree slopes, on an obvious path to the large cross. Superb views in all directions.

14: Starkenberger Hut to Neustift

From the hut descend SE bypassing the gravel track road to Schönegg. Continue SE through trees and alpine meadows along a steep well marked path to the outskirts of Neustift. Excellent scenery. Proceed along the road SE into the village square and bus stop **H** back to Innsbruck.

Stubai Glacier Tour - Höhen Weg

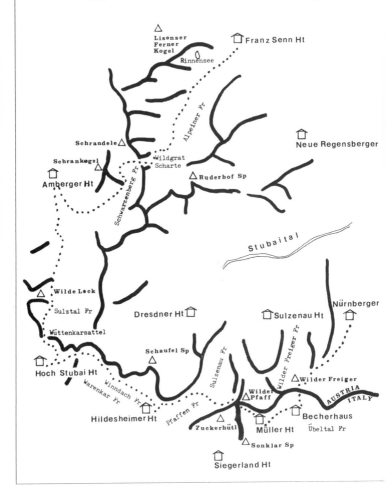

THE STUBAI GLACIER TOUR - HÖHEN WEG

GENERAL INTRODUCTION

Known in German as the Höhen Weg, this little-known tour takes in the very best of the Stubai Alps.

The route as the name implies involves much glacier work, which makes it a prerequisite to have the necessary experience and skills to deal with the great variety of terrain that will be crossed.

Though the route is primarily intended for the experienced, it is also ideal for those climbers wishing to visit the Alps for the first time. However, before doing so, each person should be familiar with the use of ice axe and crampons, be able to belay on rock and ice, have practiced Prusiking and crevasse rescue techniques, and be familiar with rope management for glacier travel.

Whilst the tour is undoubtedly tough, it is not unremittingly demanding. It will therefore suit those aspirant alpinists wishing to expand and develop their alpine experience without feeling over-committed and out of their depth - as is often the case in the higher mountains of the Western Alps. As a word of encouragement, the route has been successfully traversed by several young teenagers in the English section of the Austrian Alpine Club, though I must add that all the youngsters had received winter survival training or had attended basic rock and ice courses.

As with the Stubai Rucksack Route, the Glacier Tour is a hut to hut tour and whilst the Rucksack Route skirts around the mountains to miss the glaciers, the very essence of the glacier tour is to traverse them. The reward for the effort is the infinite variety of glacier scenery, viewed from the many peaks and passes that are crossed.

The tour starts at the Franz Senn Hut, then to the Amberger Hut via the Wildgrat Scharte, opposite the Schrankogel's north face. From the Amberger Hut, the highest hut in the Stubai, the Hoch Stubai Hut is reached via the spectacular Sulztal glacier. Thereafter, a long descending traverse of the Waren and Windach glaciers leads to the popular Hildesheimer Hut. From this premier hut the route goes into Italy via the Frontier Ridge, across the Stubai's highest peak, the Zuckerhütl and its close neighbour the Wilder Pfaff to the once derelict Müller Hut on the Austro-Italian border in the South Tyrol.

The final part of the glacier tour crosses to Übeltal glacier and the impressive Wilder Freiger to end at the Nürnberger Hut.

Six days of superb mountaineering.

ROUTE SUMMARY

page

1. Innsbruck to the Franz Senn Hut 92

    (For excursions from the Franz Senn Hut see

    Stubai Rucksack Route) 80

    Ascents of the Rinnensee, the Sommerwand and the

    Lisenser Fernerkogel, Routes 11a-11c. 80

2. Franz Senn Hut to the Amberger Hut, including ascent of

    the Schrankogel 94

3. Amberger Hut to the Hoch Stubai Hut 98

4. Hoch Stubai Hut to the Hildesheimer Hut, including

    ascent of the Schaufelspitze 101

5. Hildesheimer Hut to the Müller Hut via the Zuckerhütl and

    Wilder Pfaff 104

    5a.   Hildesheimer Hut to the Siegerland Hut 110

    5b.   Siegerland Hut to the Müller Hut,

            via the Sonklarspitze 112

6. Müller Hut to the Nürnberger Hut

    via the Wilder Freiger 115

Altitudes

Franz Senn Hut 2147m

Amberger Hut 2135m

Hoch Stubai Hut 3175m

Hildesheimer Hut 2899m

Müller Hut 3145m

Nürnberger Hut 2297m

Neustift 1000m

Wildgrat Scharte 3168m

Schrankogel 3496m

Wüttenkarsattel 3015m

Wilde Leck 3361m

Warenkarscharte 3187m

Bilstöckljoch 3128m

Schaufelspitze 3333m

Pfaffenjoch 3212m

Zuckerhütl 3505m

Pfaffensattel 3344m

Wilder Pfaff 3457m

Pfaffenneider 3136m

Wilder Freiger 3419m

Ranalt 1303m

1000m 1500m 2000m 2500m 3000m 3500m

ROUTE DESCRIPTIONS AND SKETCH MAPS

1: Innsbruck to the Franz Senn Hut via the village of Milders in the Stubaital

Innsbruck to Milders (1026m)
Regular bus service from Innsbruck. See the Stubai Rucksack Route description for the bus journey to Neder/Neustift.

Take the bus as far as Neustift, which is one stop after Neder at the start of the Rucksack Route. Neustift is the main village in the Stubaital, a little to the NE of the junction with the Oberbergtal valley.

From Neustift either:

a) Walk down the main road for $2^{1}/_{2}$km, turning right at the signpost into the cluster of chalet houses that is Milders.
b) Get off the bus, the third stop after Neustift at Bergland. Cross over the bridge and turn right immediately thereafter, walking the remaining $^{1}/_{2}$km to Milders.

Milders to the Franz Senn Hut (2147m)

Standard time:	5hrs
Distance:	11km
Ascent:	1121m

From the village square in Milders there is a regular jeep service up the Oberbergtal to the Oberiss Hut 1745m. If you have difficulty in locating the bus cum jeep stop, you should make enquiries at the Hotel Almhof Danler in the village square.

The jeep services is available at 0830, 0930 and 1530.

A taxi service is also available from the hotel for those who wish to get to the hut quickly and have sufficient funds.

Route A
For those parties wishing to enjoy the walk and get into the feel of things, follow the road from Neustift for $1^{1}/_{2}$km, signpost and waymark 131. Follow this W to miss Milders until it regains the

Milders to the Franz Senn Hut

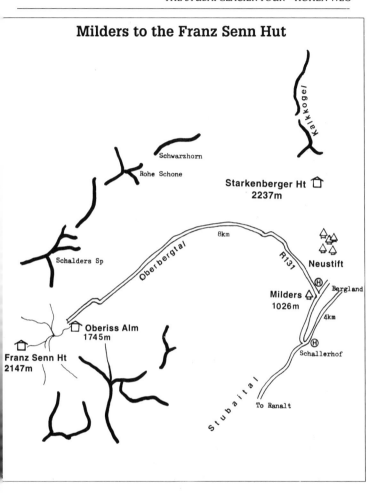

road. The route now follows the road on and off, but always adjacent to it, first to Barenbad then to Sedugg, Stocklenalm and finally Oberiss Hut, 3¹/₂ hours and 8km from Milders.

Route B

From the popular Oberiss Hut (restaurant) there is a cable-car hoist or Seilbahn for the Franz Senn Hut. For a small charge rucksacks may be hoisted the final 400 metres to the hut.

After the Oberiss Hut the path steepens in a series of zigzags rising 300m in a short distance, finally levelling out just before the hut (1¹/₂hrs).

Overall, the walk is a disappointing trudge. Since the Oberbergtal is a steep valley, the views are restricted until beyond Sedugg when parts of the Kalkkogel (Starkenberger Hut) and Schwarzhorn (Franz Senn Way) become more visible. This confinement coupled with the disadvantage of following a roadway, laden with a heavy rucksack, is not the best of mountaineering experiences. It is better to make use of the transport available and then to enjoy one of the short excursions from the hut to the Rinnensee or up the Sommerwand (see Rucksack Route tour summary).

2: Franz Senn Hut to the Amberger Hut via the Wildgrat Scharte (3168m)

Standard time:	6 hours (This is rarely achieved, allow 8 hours)
Distance:	11km
Ascent:	1021m

Crossing the stream just outside the hut, follow the left bank of Alpeiner Bach SW for 2¹/₂km, R131, until it starts to rise steeply among old glacial moraines at the foot of the Aperer Turm.

From hereabouts the scenery starts to open up, mostly dominated by the Seespitze and the icefall of the Alpeiner glacier. Continuing to follow the red waymarks, the track rises more steeply, heading SSW to gain access onto the left bank of the Alpeiner glacier at 2700m (2hrs). After kitting out with axe and crampons set off across the glacier, heading SW in a wide arc, to avoid the icefall, to a point due E of the Nordl Wildgrat Spitze at about 2900m and a group of crevasses. Now move SSW to the foot of the Sudl Wildgrat Spitze east ridge. The Wildgrat Scharte is now placed due east in an

Franz Senn Hut to the Amberger Hut

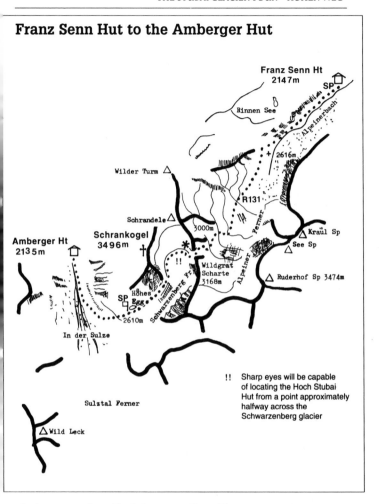

!! Sharp eyes will be capable of locating the Hoch Stubai Hut from a point approximately halfway across the Schwarzenberg glacier

obvious gap along the interconnecting ridge.

Negotiate the bergschrund, keeping close to the rocks of the east ridge, climb the slope to the col 3168m (3-4hrs). Good belay at half-height. There are spectacular views from the col of the

Ruderhofspitze; Seespitze group and the Schrankogel 3496m, the Stubai's second highest mountain with its spectacular NE face.

Scramble down rocks on the west side of the Wildgrat Scharte and cross the Schwarzenberg glacier in a wide arc to a point approximately 3100m on the Schrankogel's east flank. Crevasse danger in the centre and on the right bank. Whilst crossing the Schwarzenberg glacier, keep an eye open and recce the route to the Hoch Stubai Hut via the Sulztal glacier to the south-west. Good observers will be able to locate the hut on a knoll to the south.

Negotiating the Schrankogel lower east ridge is a grotty affair and needs much care until the path becomes obvious again. Look for cairns or marker posts.

Having gained the path at about 2800m follow the lateral moraines SW to a tiny tarn and junction with the main track up the Schrankogel, the Höhes Egg at 2610m. The path is now clearly defined heading W then NW above the marshy Sulztalbach to the Amberger Hut 2135m.

High points
An excellent day out full of scenic variety, interest and challenge. The main event of the day is crossing the Wildgrat Scharte, the view from which is superb, for it is situation type scenery as opposed to a view typical from a summit. The Scharte itself is just about big enough to accommodate a few people sitting. On one side is the expanse of glacier to the Ruderhofspitze and on the other the dominant wedge of the north-east face of the Schrankogel, offering one of the best snow climbs in the region.

Cautionary notes
The standard time for the journey is 6 hours. This is rarely achieved and many parties will take much longer. The average is about 8 hours, so you need to be on your way by 0630 hours.

Crossing the Wildgrat Scharte from the Alpeiner glacier is very much subject to seasonal change. With snow cover, the ascent is pretty straightforward. However, with minimal snow, as may exist late in the season, crossing the bergschrund can prove quite difficult and the slopes above it may be hard ice. As a precaution, enquire from the guardian at the Franz Senn Hut to make sure the col is passable or check entries in the hut book.

Ascent of the Schrankogel (3496m)

Fit climbers may find passing so close to the mountain a temptation they cannot resist. Climbing the east ridge should fulfil that need. From the point 3100m at the junction of the east ridge with the right bank of the Schwarzenberg glacier, gain the ridge and follow it to the summit.

The final 100m is usually a snow crest and may be corniced, keep N at a safe distance. In descent, either retrace your steps back down

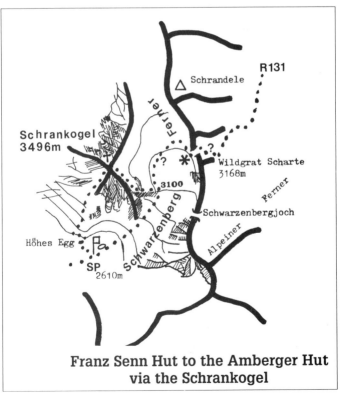

**Franz Senn Hut to the Amberger Hut
via the Schrankogel**

The NE Face of the Schrankogel from the Wildgrat Scharte

the east ridge or alternatively descend the ordinary route via the SW flank and Höhes Egg to rejoin the main track at 2610m. All in all about a 3-hour detour.

3: Amberger Hut to the Hoch Stubai Hut (3175m)

Standard time:	5 hours
Distance:	7km
Ascent:	1040m

From the hut follow R137 for about 1km south along the flat open marshy ground of In der Sulze, keeping to the left bank of the many streams that are generated by the glaciers. At 2155m signpost, the path now splits. R137 goes W to Sölden via the Atterkar Joch. Continue S heading in the direction of a large buttress, climb this in a series of zigzags to a signpost at 2280m, headed Hoch Stubai Hut

Amberger Hut to the Hoch Stubai Hut

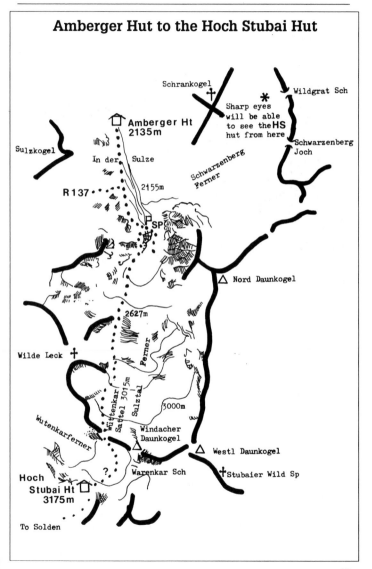

Schrankogel

Wildgrat Sch

Sharp eyes
will be able
to see the **HS**
hut from here

Schwarzenberg
Joch

⌂ Amberger Ht
2135m

Sulzkogel

In der Sulze

Schwarzenberg
Ferner

R 137

2155m

☐ SP

△ Nord Daunkogel

2627m

Wilde Leck ✝

Ferner

Wittenkar Sattel 3015m

Sulztal

3000m

Wutenkarferner

Windacher
Daunkogel

△ Westl Daunkogel

✝ Stubaier Wild Sp

?

Warenkar Sch

Hoch
Stubai Ht
3175m

To Solden

Hoch Stubai Hut from the Wütenkarsattel.
Wütenkar Glacier in the foreground with the Warenkar Scharte on the far left

and Dresdner Hut. Take the right-hand fork continuing to climb the buttress via a number of ledges until it gives way to the moraines of the left bank W of the Sulztal glacier 2627m.

Excellent view from hereabouts of the previous day's route, the Schrankogel and the icefall of the Sulztal glacier. After cramponing up get onto the glacier and continue SSW climbing the snow slopes to the Wütenkarsattel 3105m, bypassing the magnificent Wilde Leck halfway (3^{1}/$_{2}$hrs).

The Hoch Stubai Hut is now easily seen located on the opposite side of the Wütenkarferner.

From the Wütenkarsattel descend the scree slope to gain access onto the Wütenkarferner. Cross the glacier in a wide SE arc, crevasses in the centre, before ascending the final snow slope to the hut - bergschrund at about half-height.

High points
An excellent day out full of scenic interest particularly the glaciers. First and mid-way on the Sulztal glacier when the icefall is in full view and then later at the Wütenkarsattel when the Wilde Leck, Schrankogel are seen to advantage, and the size of the Sulztal can be fully appreciated.

The finale for the day is the spectacular location enjoyed by the Hoch Stubai Hut with its splendid view of the Ötztal mountains.

Cautionary notes
The main problems lie in the crossing of the Wütenkarferner when hidden crevasses in the centre of the glacier and the bergschrund just below the hut can be problematic. These potential dangers will be heightened after fresh snow falls or during bad weather.

Escape route
Descend R28 to point 2415 then R25 to Sölden.

4: Hoch Stubai Hut to the Hildesheimer Hut (2844m)

Standard time:	4 hours
Distance:	6km
Ascent:	About 400m

A route characterised by a long descending traverse. From the hut, regain the Wütenkarferner by retracing tracks across the bergschrund. Cross the glacier's upper snow slopes ENE to the Warenkar Scharte 3187m.

From the col descend steep broken ground, east, first scrambling down dubious rock then steep snow to gain the Warenkarferner glacier.

Once on the glacier proper, traverse it. First E then SE below the Westl Dunkogel, taking care to keep around the 2950m contour to a tiny col at the foot of the Stubai Wildspitze SW ridge. From hereabouts, you should be able to hear the clatter of ski-tow machinery located on the Bildstöckljoch.

Continue ESE across the Windacher , taking care to avoid

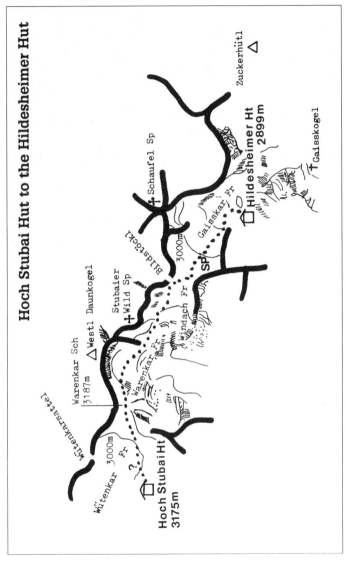

Hoch Stubai Hut to the Hildesheimer Hut

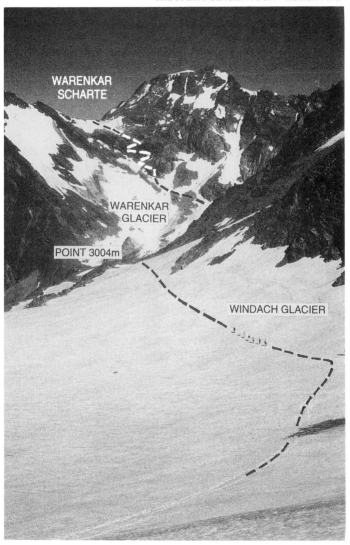

Hoch Stubai Hut to the Hildesheimer Hut.
Warenkar Scharte from the Bildstöckljoch

crevasses at 3000m whilst ascending the glacier to the col 3244m and the junction of routes joining from the Dresdner Hut.

From the Bildstöckljoch 3144m continue across the glacier SE to a col 3149m - the Eisjoch with its attendant ski-tow pylons and kiosk at the head of the Gaisskarferner.

From the Eisjoch a quick ascent can be made of the adjacent Schaufelspitze 3333m. Ascend the glacier NE to the col Isidorneider 3158m. Keep right S of the col and scramble up the SW flank (path of sorts) over loose rocks to the large summit cross (1hr).

From Eisjoch 3149m descend the Gaisskar glacier SE (marker posts) to regain the rocks at 3058m. Excellent views of the Pfaffenferner and Zuckerhütl. Continue SE following the red waymarks along the edge of the glacier, passing a small lake just before the hut.

High points
Not as spectacular as the previous day's outing but still full of challenge with some good views of the Ötztal.

The area around the Bildstöckl and Eisjoch was at one time a splendid alpine plateau. Unfortunately, it is now spoiled by the proliferation of ski-tow machinery put up in the early eighties for summer skiers. Some consolation is gained by the view of the Wilder Pfaff and Zuckerhütl from the Schaufelspitze.

Cautionary notes
Whilst the route has no technical difficulties, care is needed in descending the steep ground from the Warenkar Scharte onto the Warenkarferner. The only crevasse danger is just below the Bildstöckl. However, the route is very problematic in bad weather when route finding is difficult.

5: Hildesheimer Hut to the Müller Hut (3145m)

Standard time:	6 hours
Distance:	7km
Ascent:	720m

Hildesheimer Hut to the Müller Hut

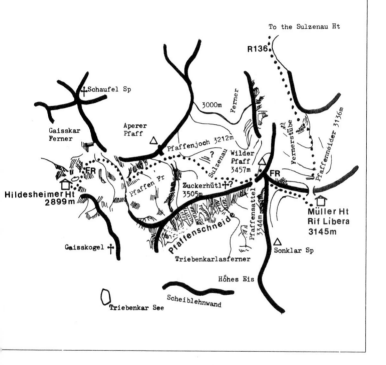

Perhaps the finest day's alpine promenade of the whole glacier tour.

From the hut, signpost, descend the path NE to a small lake just below the hut. Then descend E diagonally across a steep rock buttress with fixed ropes, down onto the old moraines of the Pfaffen glacier.

Cross below the foot of the Gaisskar glacier NE, contouring E across scree and snow slopes to the base of the Aperer Pfaff. Splendid view of the Pfaffen glacier's icefall and Gaisskogel.

PFAFFEN JOCH

to the ZUCKERHUTL

PFAFFEN GLACIER

Pfaffenschneide from the Hildesheimer Hut

Ascend the right bank, N of the Pfaffenferner, keeping close to the rocks of the Aperer Pfaff to the Pfaffenjoch 3212m (2hrs). Superb views in all direction. Cross the head of the col E onto the upper slopes of the Sulzenauferner. Cross the glacier SE to the Pfaffensattel 3344m, avoiding several crevasses and bypassing the Zuckerhütl's magnificent north face en-route. At the col rucksacks may be left whilst completing the climb.

From the col climb the right-hand snow ridge keeping to the northern side of the mountain, to the Zuckerhütl's (Sugarloaf) large metal summit cross 3505m. The ridge is frequently corniced and steepens considerably near the top. Descend via the same route retracing steps to the Pfaffensattel.

Alternatively from the Pfaffenjoch the Zuckerhütl may be traversed via the Pfaffenschneide; this is recommended. From the col, go onto the upper slopes of the Sulzenau glacier and climb the snow slopes SE, keeping on the north side of a rock outcrop to point 3366m. Cross the col SE and scramble up the rocky ridge to the Pfaffenschneide 3498m. Descend the Pfaffenschneide's east ridge to a broad snow-covered col 3432m at the junction of the Zuckerhütl's west ridge. Climb the ridge, often a snow crest, keeping to the left on the north side of the mountain to the summit ($1^{1}/_{2}$hrs).

From the summit descend the steep east ridge, snow-covered and corniced to the Pfaffensattel ($^{1}/_{2}$hr).

From the Pfaffensattel climb the Wilder Pfaff (Wild Priest) by continuing up the snow-covered west ridge keeping on the north side to the summit (3458m) with its summit cairn and rudimentary wooden cross in about 1 hour.

From the summit, the Müller Hut is clearly visible at the foot of the east ridge a little beyond the Pfaffenneider. From the summit descend the steep east ridge, first down airy blank slabs protected by fixed ropes, giving way to good scrambling over granite blocks, exposed in parts. Continue down the ridge keeping to its south side until a snow crest is reached at point 3270m. Get onto the Übeltalferner hereabouts continuing E to the Pfaffenneider and the Müller Hut ($1^{1}/_{2}$hrs).

High points
Not surprisingly almost everyone staying at the Hildesheimer Hut

will have in mind an ascent of the Stubai's highest mountain the Zuckerhütl 3505m. The mountain is best seen from the Grosser Trögler on the Stubai Rucksack Route, from where its pseudonym of Sugarloaf is apparent. Also apparent from this vantage point is a spectacular view of the Zuckerhütl's glaciers and the icefalls off the Sulzenauferner and Fernerstübe.

The route comprises some first class glacier scenery particularly at the foot of the Pfaffenferner to pass the icefall, then later at the Pfaffenjoch as the route opens up to the great expanse of the upper Sulzenauferner revealing the Zuckerhütl's north face.

Whilst the normal route up the mountain via the Pfaffensattel is excellent the route over the Pfaffenschneide is highly recommended. Since it is only marginally harder and a little longer, it should present no real increase in difficulty. This variation provides some real good alpine situations particularly point 3366m and the broad col 3422m which are dramatically exposed on both sides of the mountain.

Obviously the view from the Zuckerhütl's summit is superb, particularly of its close neighbours the Sonklarspitze 3467m with its sculptured east face and Triebenkarlasferner. Similarly the Wilder Pfaff from whose own summit is revealed its steep precipitous north ridge and the reasons why it is called the Wild Priest. Further afield are the ever popular Wilder Freiger and Schrankogel, whilst on the horizon are the mountains of the Ötztal in the west, the Zillertal to the east and the Dolomites to the south.

The route is extremely popular and one to savour. You are advised to be on your way no later than 0600 hours to enjoy this excellent alpine promenade and before the sun has the chance to soften up the snow slopes below the Pfaffenjoch and Pfaffensattel.

Cautionary notes
Because of the nature of the route and the remoteness of the Müller Hut, it should only be undertaken in reasonably settled weather. Though route finding is not particularly difficult in good weather, since the route is often a well beaten trail, nevertheless in mist and cloud crossing the glacier from the Pfaffenjoch to the Pfaffensattel can be problematic as can attempts to reverse the route. During such conditions attempts to climb the mountain via its corniced ridges

should be avoided due to the very real danger of walking off the mountain. Obviously these dangers will be further heightened after fresh snow or when there are whiteouts or storm conditions exist.

Normally most crevasse dangers are obvious, first at the foot of the Pfaffenjoch, then between the Pfaffenjoch and Pfaffensattel, and finally just before the Müller Hut.

During actual climbing care should be exercised in descending from the summit of the Wilder Pfaff down the steep rock buttress via its fixed ropes which can be awkward when wet or frost-covered. Similarly in ascent and descent of the Zuckerhütl's corniced east ridge and when crossing the tiny col between the Pfaffenschneide and the Zuckerhütl.

Escape route
In very severe weather the correct decision is to descend from the Hildesheimer Hut to Sölden in the Ötztal valley, first by R102 on the Aschenbrenner Way to Gaisstal at the head of the Windachtal, then follow R102 down the valley along the Central Alpine Way.

East ridge of the Zuckerhutl from the Wilder Pfaff. Sulzenau Glacier and Pfaffenjoch on the far right

Alternatively, when low cloud persists, either proceed to the Siegerland Hut by the route described over the Gamsplatzl, or proceed to the Dresdner Hut by retracing steps to the Bildstöckl, then reversing the route described for the Schaufelspitze.

Alternative Poor Weather Routes

The following two route descriptions, Hildesheimer Hut to the Müller Hut via the Siegerland Hut and Sonklarspitze are provided as a viable alternative in bad weather - as a means of buying some time. Also, to provide that much needed psychological change of scene moral booster when being confined for more than a day or so at the Hildesheimer Hut. Whilst not on the glacier tour proper, crossing the Sonklarspitze is a worthy alternative to the Zuckerhütl-Wilder Pfaff traverse.

Unfortunately, it is not an easy undertaking and should equally be avoided in poor weather. Therefore, during bad weather, you must decide either to sit out the weather at the Hildesheimer Hut and wait for conditions to improve before attempting the Zuckerhütl, or to move on to the Siegerland Hut and gamble on the weather improving to cross the Sonklarspitze. In very poor weather the right decision from either hut is to descend to Sölden in the Ötztal valley.

However, should the weather forecast improve, making the route over the Sonklarspitze possible, you may consider spending a second night at the Müller Hut and reversing the route to the Zuckerhütl via the Wilder Pfaff.

These notes are to help you decide!

5a: Hildesheimer Hut to the Siegerland Hut (2710m)

Standard time:	3 hours
Distance:	4km
Ascent:	120m

From the hut descend the rocky outcrop of the Gaisskar, heading SE waymark 140, to the foot of the buttress. Cross the boulder field, crossing the Gaisskbach stream by a rickety bridge **B** at 2700m.

Continue S, up the flank of the Gaisskogel by a series of zigzags over boulders and large blocks to the Gamsplatzl 3019m, a small col at the foot of the Gaisskogel's N ridge (1¹/₂hrs).

Super view of the Öztal and Sonklarspitze west face. From the col descend steep ground of rock and scree of the Gamsfalle SE to immediately N of the Triebenkar See 2655m. The path continues SE just above the snout of the Triebenkarlasferner then turns S along the Scheiblehnwand to a small col 2656. The path then resume a SE direction to the hut (1¹/₂hrs).

Hildesheimer Hut to the Siegerland Hut.
Siegerland Hut to the Müller Hut / Rifugio Libera

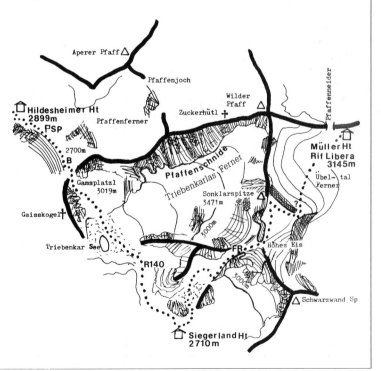

Botzer and the Übeltal Glacier from the Müller Hut

High points
A pleasant walk, though obviously lacking the excitement of the previous day's promenades. Nevertheless, the route has some points of merit, particularly the view of the Sonklarspitze west face and steep Treibenkarlas glacier - a superb climb in its own right. Then once at the Siegerland Hut, there is the view of the Ötztal and its highest mountain, the Wildspitze.

Cautionary notes
The route has no particular difficulties and is well marked with the usual daubs of red paint throughout. However, since it is likely to be undertaken in less than favourable weather, parties should endeavour to stick strictly to the path to locate the bridge over the Gaissbach stream and in descending the steep slopes of the Gamsfalle. The Gamsplatzl should be avoided during storm conditions due to the possibility of lightning.

5b: Siegerland Hut to the Müller Hut via the Sonklarspitze (3471m)

Standard time:	5 hours
Distance:	4km
Ascent:	761m

From behind the hut, ascend rough broken ground heading NNE to a tiny lake at 2800m - waymarked sparingly with cairns.

The route continues N over glacial debris into a broad couloir, between the Scheiblehnwand and the SW ridge from the Höhes Eis. Proceed up the couloir to the snow field, continuing to gain height to around the 3000m. Hereabouts, the route turns E, over boulders and slabs to the SW ridge 3017m (1¹/₂hrs). Continue along the ridge, airy and exposed in places, to its end. Climb the snow crest of the Höhes Eis 3388m, keeping on the south side of the ridge, to avoid the steep northern edge of the Triebenkarlasferner, which is often corniced. From the Höhes Eis, continue along the upper snow slope first E, then N to point 3432m, crevasses, and on to the large flat top summit 3467m (1¹/₂hrs). Excellent views.

From the summit, the Müller Hut and Becherhaus will be clearly visible across the Übeltal glacier. Descend SE to the top of the E ridge, an ill-defined area where the NE and SE flanks converge. Descend steep broken ground, grotty in places, keeping on the N of the ridge, cairns in places, until it's possible to get onto the upper

Müller Hut to the Nürnberger Hut.
Siegerland Hut to the Müller Hut via the Sonklarspitze

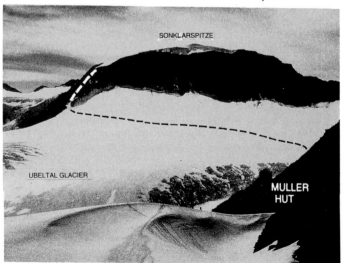

edge of the Übeltal glacier (1hr). Bergschrund at the foot of the ridge and one usually at 3250m. Cross the glacier NNE, crevasses, to the hut (1hr).

High points

An excellent route and equally as challenging as the Zuckerhütl-Wilder Pfaff traverse. Though the initial start is a disappointing trudge over scrappy glacial debris, once on the SW ridge interest abounds. First with good scrambling, airy and exposed in places, providing excellent opportunities for action photos. The rock ridge then gives way to the snow crest of the Höhes Eis, which though short is quite steep and spectacular.

The Sonklarspitze summit is more of a flat top with no obvious cairn or summit cross. The views are excellent, particularly of the Zuckerhütl, Wilder Freiger and the mountains of the Stubai's South Tyrol. There is also good opportunity to recce the route across the Übeltal glacier to the Müller Hut and the route up the Wilder Freiger. Parties who may be tempted to proceed along the north ridge to the Wilder Pfaff should note that the route is graded PD plus with pitches of III, though not sustained. The rock is of Stubai quality and not very good. In descent, it is possible to avoid most of the E ridge by getting onto the glacier around the 3350m contour, followed by two abseils, which usually gets one across the offending bergschrund. Thereafter, the crossing of the Übeltal glacier, though heavily crevassed, is quite straightforward and full of scenic interest being surrounded by high mountains. This is a superb day out set amid high mountains. You are advised to be on your way by 7am.

Cautionary notes

Though the Sonklarspitze is regularly climbed from the Siegerland Hut, route marking using the customary cairns and rocks daubed with red paint is generally poor. This will be experienced first in ascending the broad couloir of the Höhes Eis and then later in descending the E ridge onto the Übeltal glacier.

Route finding difficulties will be further hindered in mist when trying to locate the E ridge corridor from the Sonklarspitze summit. Whilst crevasses are not normally a problem, the bergschrund at foot of the E ridge onto the Übeltal glacier can be difficult to cross late in season, by which time it is usually quite large.

Overall, as previously noted, the Sonklarspitze is as equally serious an undertaking as the Zuckerhütl, with perhaps more general route finding difficulties. It should therefore be avoided if the weather is generally poor.

6: Müller Hut to the Nürnberger Hut (2280m)

Standard time:	5 hours
Distance:	6km
Ascent:	275m via the Wilder Freiger 3419m

From the Müller Hut a choice of routes is available to climb the Wilder Freiger 3419m.

South-West Ridge

From the hut traverse the rocks adjacent to the hut to regain the Übeltal glacier at 3152m. Proceed east for a short distance then head NE, keeping close to the rocks of the SW ridge to point 3228m. Either gain the SW ridge here or continue up the glacier to point 3264m before getting onto the ridge. Climb the ridge, rock in its entirety with some dubious fixed ropes, to the summit with its large wooden cross (2hrs).

South-West Flank

Get onto the Übeltal glacier as described and proceed to point 3228m. Continue up the glacier's right bank, E, keeping parallel to the SW ridge passing point 3264m. Make a slight detour NE away from the SW ridge until just right of the Wilder Freiger's summit to avoid a bank of crevasses on the 3300m contour. Continue up the glacier to the foot of an obvious snow couloir. Cross the bergschrund and climb the steepish snow slope to its end, finally scrambling up rocks to the summit (2hrs).

From the summit cross, descend SE keeping on the N of the ridge to the Signalgipfel 3392m with its unmistakable derelict customs hut. Continue NE over broken ground, frequently snow-covered to 3324m at the junction with the Wilder Freiger's east

Müller Hut to the Nürnberger Hut

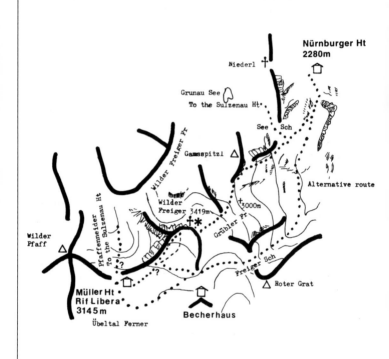

ridge. Get back onto the glacier proper and descend the snow crest NNE to 3222m. Follow the obvious rock ridge to a col south of the Gamsspitzl. Excellent view in all directions. Scramble down the rocks and cross the patch of snow (which may be iced late in season) NE to its end. Regain the rocks, good path and waymarked, continuing NE to the See Scharte 2762m at the junction of routes with the Sulzenau Hut.

From the See Scharte, continue NE over rocks and broken

Müller Hut to the Nürnberger Hut.
Botzer, the Becherhaus from the Übeltal Glacier

ground always well marked to the Nürnberger Hut (2-3hrs).

High points
The initial section of the route is mostly influenced by the extent of the Übeltal glacier and immediate scenery into the South Tyrol, dominated by the multi buttressed Botzer, a fine mountain in its own right. Parties will also be curious to see what is happening at the Becherhaus, the Müller Hut's close neighbour and previously the highest hut in the Stubai, until forfeited to Italy after World War I.

Once on the SW ridge, the scenery dramatically opens up, as does the degree of exposure on both sides of the ridge, reinforcing the need to take care.

All this pales in comparison once on the summit of the Wilder Freiger 3419m. For the Freiger is the epitome of most climbers' ideal mountain, set as it is amongst the Stubai's largest glaciers. The Freiger is a beautiful snow-covered mountain with perhaps the most extensive view in the Stubai. Equally because the normal way up the mountain from the Nürnberger Hut is straightforward, the Freiger is perhaps justifiably the most popular mountain in the Stubai. Not surprisingly on a good day many parties will climb the mountain to enjoy the views across the South Tyrol as far south as the Dolomites and Marmolata. In the west are the Ötztal and the other Stubai peaks, Zuckerhütl, Wilde Leck and around to the Ruderhofspitze. To the east, the magnificent Zillertal and Venediger,

Müller Hut to the Nürnberger Hut. Ascent of the Wilder Freiger. Botzer, the Becherhaus Übertal Glacier from the Wilder Freiger's summit

whilst on the northern horizon the Kalkkogel and Karwendal groups will easily be seen. Also visible for those with keen eyesight is the Starkenberger Hut above Neustift.

Leaving the summit behind, the scenery remains excellent with a couple of places worthy of note. First, just north of the Gamsspitzl, there is a spectacular view of the Wilder Freiger and its attendant glacier. Aspirant alpinists may ponder its complexity and judge whether they have sufficient skills to negotiate such complex glacier terrain, first climbed over 100 years ago. Then somewhat lower, the col of the See Scharte, at the junction of routes from the Sulzenau Hut, provides a similar view with the twin peaks of the Feuerstein dominating the scene. But equally important is the profusion of alpine flowers that grow around the col, particularly the vivid blue gentian.

Overall, a superb day out amid fine alpine scenery full of interest and challenge and perhaps only eclipsed by the traverse of the Zuckerhütl.

Cautionary notes
Because of the expanse of glaciers, warm air from the south can quickly condense into thick mist, making route finding particularly

Müller Hut to the Nürnberger Hut. Ascent of the Wilder Freiger

difficult on the Übeltal glacier and when descending from the summit to the See Scharte.

Under normal circumstances, route finding from the summit is not particularly difficult as the Freiger is an extremely popular mountain and the track across the head of the Wilder Freiger Ferner and Grüblferner will be a well defined snow trough. However, in mist and after fresh snow has fallen, the route may not be obvious. You should stick strictly to the route via the Signalgipfel and avoid the temptation to cut the corner of the Wilder Freiger's glacier which suddenly steepens and leads to a labyrinth of crevasses.

The ascent of the SW ridge is straightforward with no specific climbing difficulties. However, the rock in places is suspect and needs to be handled with care. Similarly, the fixed wire ropes are of dubious quality and best avoided. The ridge must be avoided at all costs during storm conditions as it is frequently hit by lightning strike.

Those parties preferring an ascent of the mountain via the upper Übeltal glacier will find the crux of the route to be in crossing the bergschrund and in climbing the snow couloir. Obviously this section of the route is subject to seasonal change and can vary dramatically from being a straightforward snow slope to one of hard ice, requiring good ice axe and cramponing techniques.

Overall, the route is a fine weather route and one to be avoided on a falling barometer or dodgy weather forecast.

Escape routes from the Müller Hut
Because of the hut's remoteness there are no easy routes down the mountain.

The most direct route is via the Fernerstübe, R136, to the Sulzenau Hut. Allow a minimum of 5 hours.

From the Müller Hut, descend to the Pfaffenneider. Descend the steep rocky slope to gain the Fernerstübe glacier. Get onto the glacier and descend the short steep snow slope, often iced to a bergschrund. Cross the bergschrund, often quite difficult if the snow bridge has collapsed, to the glacier.

Continue on the right bank of the glacier, N, to just above the icefall. Negotiate the short icefall, look for marker poles NW. Proceed NNW closer to the edge of the glacier's right bank under the Aperer Freiger. Leave the glacier at 2700m, following a well defined moraine NE to the Blaue Lacke and onto the hut.

Alternatively, descend to the Nürnberger Hut: an exercise in route finding ability, but without any serious glacier obstacles. Allow 5 hours. From the Müller Hut, return to the Pfaffenneider and get onto the Übeltal glacier. Cross the glacier E, crevasses midway, to the col just below the Becherhaus. You may wish to spend a night here, the Stubai's previously highest hut 3190m, if the weather has deteriorated further.

From the col 3157m, descend steep rocks to get back onto the Übeltal glacier. Traverse the glacier E, maintaining the 3000m contour to the Freiger Scharte 3025m. Continue by descending the Grüblferner, first NE to 2800m between the Höhewand and a rock island, then NNE and finally N in the direction of the Urfallspitze, leaving the glacier at around 2500m. Thereafter, the route is waymarked to the hut.